27 VIEWS OF WILMINGTON

RALEIGH

OAKDALE CEMETERY

THALIAN HALL

AIRLIE GARDENS

FRONT St.

THIRD STREET

- M - A - R - K - E - T

UNCW

BEACH

BEACH

VENUS FLYTRAPS

BEACH

COURTHOUSE

BEACH

BELLAMY MANSION

27 Views of WILMINGTON

The Port City in Prose & Poetry

Introduction by Celia Rivenbark

eno
publishers

27 Views of Wilmington: The Port City in Prose & Poetry
Introduction by Celia Rivenbark
© Eno Publishers 2015
All rights reserved

publishers

Eno Publishers
P.O. Box 158, Hillsborough, North Carolina 27278
www.enopublishers.org

ISBN: 978-0-9896092-3-4
ISBN-10: 0-9896092-3-5
Library of Congress Control Number: 2015943342
Printed in the United States
10 9 8 7 6 5 4 3 2 1

Cover illustration by Daniel Wallace, Chapel Hill, North Carolina
Design and typesetting by Horse & Buggy Press, Durham, North Carolina

Publisher's Acknowledgments

Eno Publishers wishes to thank Gita Schonfeld, Speed Hallman, Caitlin Whalen, Meg Williamson, Sophie Shaw, Laura Lacy, and Adrienne Fox for their great work in making 27 *Views of Wilmington* happen, and Daniel Wallace for his imaginative illustration of the Port City.

A huge thank you to our Port City authors and to the Introduction writer, Celia Rivenbark, who have created a literary mosaic of Wilmington, present and past.

Permissions & Acknowledgments

Bertha Boykin Todd's essay "A Successful Coup d'What?" cites material from *Moving Forward Together: A Community Remembers 1898*, edited by Rhonda Bellamy and Si Cantwell, published by the 1898 Memorial Foundation (November 2008).

Gwenyfar's essay "Restorations" is adapted from a story that originally appeared in *Salt* magazine (September 2014).

Virginia Holman's essay "The Face of the River" is adapted from a story of the same name that first appeared in *Salt* magazine (June 2014).

Sheila Webster Boneham's poem "Spin" was published in *The Written River* (Summer 2014).

Robert Anthony Siegel's essay "Ode to My Backyard" originally appeared in the *Oxford American* (Spring 2006).

Ashley Wahl's essay "Ballads of Change" is adapted from a piece that originally appeared in *Salt* magazine (April 2015).

Wendy Brenner's essay "Love & Death in the Cape Fear Serpentarium" has been published in the *Oxford American* (Spring 2005) and was included in *The Best American Magazine Writing 2006*.

Nan Graham's essay "Esther, Andy & Me" is adapted from a story that first appeared in *Salt* magazine (April 2014).

Some passages in John Jeremiah Sullivan's "Animals" are adapted from works that were first published in the *Oxford American* and in the *Financial Times*.

Michael White's poem, "Coup," has been published in the *North Carolina Literary Review* and in his book, *Vermeer in Hell*.

Table of Contents

⚓ A PLACE CALLED HOME

⚓ CLOSE-UPS

⚓ A WORLD APART

⚓ STREET SCENES

VIEWS FROM BEFORE

VIEWS FROM 1898 & BEYOND

VIEWS IN FICTION

Preface

27 Views of Wilmington is just that: twenty-seven reflections by twenty-seven local writers of life in the Port City, present and past. In story, essay, and poem, Wilmington-area viewers capture some aspect of the community they call home.

In some views, Wilmington is front and center; in others, the city serves as a backdrop. Some celebrate the Port City, its traditions, charms, and natural beauty; others delve into its complexities—its struggles with growth, inequality, cultural change, the past. It's revealing that five of our twenty-seven writers tackle the 1898 insurrection. The healing continues. Still others offer personal stories of the downs and ups and in-betweens of life in their home, native or adopted.

This local anthology offers a literary landscape of Wilmington that spans generations, ethnicities, life experiences, genres to create a sense of place, the spirit of place that, we hope, will reinforce, inform, and possibly inspire more views.

Enjoy.

Elizabeth Woodman
Eno Publishers | Summer 2015

Introduction

WILMINGTON, NORTH CAROLINA, IS A quirky, unpretentious little city where in one downtown block you might spot Robert Downey Jr. sipping chai tea followed minutes later by a teenager wearing a hoop skirt and full-on belle costume "on account of it's beautiful." What's not to love?

I mention Downey Jr. because he was "Iron Man" here, but he is by no means the only big-time movie star to work in Wilmington. Hundreds have, because (1) we have an amazing movie studio and (2) on account of it's beautiful here.

My lifelong love affair with the Port City isn't some shallow eighth-grade infatuation. I loved her when she was, frankly, down on her luck. Think of the Sixties and Seventies: a decrepit downtown, integration struggles, race riots, low-wage jobs and not even many of those, not her best moment.

I grew up about an hour north in rural Duplin County but made the trek "to town" every single Saturday to buy groceries at Winn-Dixie ("a real grocery store," proclaimed my mother). We always made a stop in a sketchy bookstore on Princess Street downtown, and sometimes I would sit in the car while Mama shopped for a new Perry Mason mystery. I didn't care much for the store but I did like to watch the fat old orange tomcat that snored on a stack of girlie magazines displayed in the front window. Non-Baptists had to lift up that old wheezy tom to retrieve their porn, a big price to pay since fat cat had one tooth left and knew how to use it.

One Saturday, Mama and Daddy left me to sit in their aircraft carrier of an Oldsmobile while they shopped. They'd parked right outside the old WGNI radio studios downtown. Unaware that the DJ could see me,

I gave quite a spirited sing-along to a Monkees' song playing on the car radio, complete with hairbrush microphone.

"Daydream Believer," said the DJ, his voice all whiskey and honey. "That song goes out to the little girl singing along in the back seat of a Delta 88 right here in front of the radio station!"

Well, I 'bout died. The city I loved had made me famous for nine seconds. I would never turn my back on it.

Back then, as its downtown grew scarily seedy and those mossy mansions on Front Street looked as if they'd topple into the Cape Fear River if you leaned on them hard, I had a feeling the worm would turn and Wilmington would be restored to her rightful place.

And, verily, it has happened.

For a long time associated with racial violence and injustice, from the Insurrection of 1898 up to the Wilmington Ten in 1971, this Southern city badly needed to change its ways. Gradually, it happened. My town has evolved into a more tolerant, peaceful, and just community. And, by revitalizing downtown, and promoting the natural beauty of the area, natives and visitors alike have begun to see Wilmington in a new way.

This is not to say that everything's perfect now. Of course it's not. But it's known more as a vacation, filmmaking, and foodie destination than for its bitter and complicated past. Thanks be to God and a handful of true visionaries.

Wilmington has morphed into a progressive, vibrant, artsy city with the great good fortune to be located smack in between the river and sea, and the wisdom to make the most of that fact. And twenty-seven of our authors capture the city, past and present, in 27 *Views of Wilmington: The Port City in Prose & Poetry.*

In these pages you will laugh at the image of the foul-mouthed Azalea Queen Esther Williams, shocking her tenderhearted Queen's Court. You will chuckle at the wacky world of beach trailer-park chic at a Carolina Beach dive bar. You might mist up a bit at the memory of one trailing spouse from San Francisco who threw up as soon as she saw her new home. What a revelation it was when she came to love our town fiercely. The large, loving, and wildly hospitable family on Queen Street will make you crave clam fritters and backyard tater salad, we promise.

Wilmington is quaint no more. The city's population has exploded: 45 percent growth since 2000 to slightly more than 110,000 residents today, making it North Carolina's eighth largest city.

At one time, Wilmington was a railroad town in a big way. From 1840 until the dark day in 1960 when Atlantic Coast Line Railroad suddenly moved its headquarters to Jacksonville, Fla., railroading was the town's biggest industry. A lot of old-timers still hang their heads at the memory of all those jobs disappearing overnight. Some locals followed the company south. The town's economy and lifelong friendships between neighbors were huge casualties of the move.

But Wilmington is a city that bounces back, sometimes quickly, other times not so fast, because in the South we are, sometimes rightfully, accused of moving as fast as molasses going uphill on a windy day.

Its quirky Southern nature makes Wilmington embrace tall tales, telling and retelling the grandchildren about the time in 1922 when Topsy the elephant broke away from a visiting circus and terrorized the town (well, more like meandered around it) for the better part of three days.

To this day, locals will recall Hurricane Hazel's hateful visit in October of 1954, almost always including the part about the sleeping couple who simply rode out the storm atop the waves on their mattress.

And that tradition continues in these pages. We'll remind you that our Cape Fear area is the only place in the world where the carnivorous plant, the Venus flytrap, grows naturally. A meat-eating plant. Wrap your brain around that for a minute or ten.

Today Wilmington natives, or near-natives like me, jokingly wonder if we haven't gone overboard in welcoming the world. I remember the first time I heard a friend explain to a visitor from the Northeast why Landfall, a gated community bordering the Intracoastal Waterway, had such a high fence around its perimeter. "Oh that? That's where we keep our Yankees." It was said with nary a trace of a smile, which made it all the funnier.

Interestingly, Landfall, as Wilmington's largest "Yankee containment area and country club," has a main road running through it named after the Italian explorer Giovanni da Verrazzano, the first European to see the area's charms back in 1524 (even if he did think it was China at first). He found an area full of indigenous people, and he happily recorded in his diary that "The natives are friendly here."

And we are, mostly. But in the eternal clash between the back-then and the here-now, we like to remind new residents who ask how long it will be before they are really, truly considered Southerners that "just because a cat has her kittens in the oven, it don't mean they're biscuits."

Sure, we have a popular restaurant (Casey's Buffet) that still serves chitlins but we also have a startling number of craft breweries, fair-trade coffeehouses, and, God help us, gluten-free and vegan cafes. And plenty of highly educated and extraordinarily talented waiters and waitresses who are in Wilmington for the theater life or in hopes of being cast in the dramas, sitcoms, and movies made here. We have an opera, a university, a symphony, and, by the end of 2015, a gorgeous fine arts auditorium big enough to lure those big names we've been traveling to Raleigh-Durham to see.

In Wilmington, it is not at all unusual for the person who served you a goat-cheese tart for lunch downtown to be the same face you see that night in an episode of *Sleepy Hollow*.

And while a shortsighted N.C. General Assembly did vote in 2014 to drastically reduce film incentive money, it was heartening to note that CBS's *Under the Dome* came back anyway for its second season because this is a great film town with world-class film crews and every damn body knows that except a few pea-brained legislators. Okay, more than a few.

Just on my downtown block alone, at least a dozen movies and TV shows have been filmed. At one point, I found myself an unpaid extra just hanging out my sheets on the backyard clothesline. You're welcome, *One Tree Hill*.

Old South meets new at every corner in my town and that is part of Wilmington's grand seduction. At a recent yard sale to raise money for a local elementary school, new neighbors from San Francisco introduced themselves and commented on how surprised they were to already feel at home in Wilmington. Happens all the time.

While it's unbecoming to brag, it's hard to be humble when you have such fine weather and clean beaches that you're rated among the world's best by people who keep track of that sort of thing.

In 2014 *USA Today* readers voted our riverfront the prettiest in the entire nation. This mile-long walkway has breathtaking sunset views of the *USS Battleship North Carolina* and is flanked by scores of shops and restaurants. For most of the year, a farmer's market sets up shop on the riverfront drawing hundreds every Saturday to a down-home mix of everything from snake plants ("mother-in-law's tongue") to homemade oatmeal soap to tomatoes as big as a baby's head. Sometimes it's hard to remember that if you travel just a few miles inland, you'll find yourself in deep country, far removed from this uber trendy spot that even has buskers. Buskers!!!!

Our average year-round temperature of 64 is one of the reasons Wilmington has several triathlons and marathons every year as well as international surfing competitions and well-used bike trails and public parks.

If you want to know if someone's a local or a transplant, watch their reaction when the Weather Channel, covering one of our occasional, ill-mannered hurricanes, calls us "Cape Fear, N.C." *Ugh.* Strictly speaking, it is the Cape Fear region and sits on the Cape Fear River but Cape Fear, N.C.? Just no. (Historyheads, take note: The area got the name in 1585 when the British ship *Tiger* nearly wrecked off its coast proclaiming it a "cape of feare.")

Wilmington was founded in 1740 and named after a British earl who was friends with Colonial Governor Gabriel Johnston. It had been called other names including New Liverpool, Newton, and New Carthage, but apparently they didn't stick. Someone wanted to make nice-nice and

Wilmington was incorporated, joining Edenton and New Bern to the northeast as a center of commerce.

Thirty years later, John Burgwin, a wealthy merchant and planter, built a house on the site of an old jail. If you take the popular Ghost Walk of Old Wilmington tour of the immaculately restored house-slash-prison, they'll tell you the basement is haunted. I believe it.

There are lots of opportunities to see Wilmington's past up close and personal. Gracious antebellum mansions have been restored and live again as bed-and-breakfasts. Others are open for tours, and you really can't visit here without taking in our Oakdale Cemetery at the end of North Fifteenth Street. (A friend protested when a national company built an assisted-living facility here and named it Oakdale. What?!? Eventually, the name was changed because, honestly, you can't expect the family matriarch to relax in a home that shares its name with a cemetery, even if it is the oldest and most prestigious in the area.)

Oakdale Cemetery, three blocks from my house, is where I strolled my infant daughter nearly twenty years ago, pausing with three other neighborhood moms to nurse our babies while propped on tombstones marking the graves of yellow fever victims (more than six hundred died here during an epidemic in 1862). Most of Wilmington's first families are buried here and, to this day, there will be the slightest raising of an eyebrow if you admit that you own a plot in the new section. Pity.

I told someone this story and they said we nursing moms had defiled Oakdale Cemetery, which told me they clearly weren't from around here. The South adores the incongruity of decay and new life. How better to illustrate this than by four mothers nursing four fussy babies while balanced on an ancient cemetery wall?

One does what one has to do. Besides, babies or not, it is one of the prettiest places to take a walk alone with your thoughts in all of Wilmington, a sort of Southern version of Père Lachaise Cemetery in Paris. And while we don't have Jim Morrison's famous grave at Oakdale, did I mention you can visit the grave of the young woman who died at sea en route to Wilmington and was embalmed in a barrel of whiskey?

Speaking of notables, you may not realize how many famous folk grew up here—David Brinkley (Oakdale, check), the late Charles Kuralt, Charlie Daniels, Meadowlark Lemon (of Harlem Globetrotters' fame), the late Lincoln Memorial architect Henry Bacon, Michael Jordan (and, no, he wasn't cut from his Laney High School team; that's a vicious rumor), and the late Don Payne, legendary writer of *The Simpsons.* Yes. Wilmington gave the world Homer Simpson. You're welcome.

Wilmington loves a parade and our North Carolina Azalea Festival, brought to life in these pages by Nan Graham, is legendary. Here's where you'll see those hoop-skirted high school belles and a bunch of really well-dressed, drunk people at the annual invitation-only garden party at Airlie Gardens.

There's a fabulous holiday flotilla the Saturday after Thanksgiving where you can see revelers a-Wassailing aboard every type of sailing vessel from mighty yachts to lowly johnboats, all festooned in blinking holiday lights.

And until it died from entirely natural causes, the World's Largest Living Christmas Tree near downtown's center drew hundreds of thousands to Wilmington.

I've spent half a century watching my favorite city come into her own. And it makes me smile to think that the very spot where that asthmatic old tomcat once slept on smut magazines is a stone's throw from a trendy tapas restaurant today. Tapas is a word that cranky natives like me believe is Spanish for "still gonna have to eat a Pop-Tart when I get home," but they're a nice little tide-me-over, I suppose.

If I'm trying to think of one place where old and new Wilmington mesh completely, I always come back to Rx, a restaurant at the intersection of Castle Street and Fifth Avenue (an area known by the natives only as Dry Pond) in the old Hall's Drug Store. Hall's wasn't just a drugstore; it was a center of political wisdom and had the best grilled cheese and orangeade ever. It's fitting that Rx has pretty much left the exterior alone. A fine new chef has migrated upstream from Charleston and oversees a selection of the finest seafood and also, well, fried Buffalo pig's ears. Shut up; they're amazing.

Incidentally, a Charleston chef is a plum for us because we have similar vibes and ingredients but we're just smaller and, occasionally, this grates.

We have a lovely bridge but it's no Ashley Cooper. And, truth be told, the Cape Fear Bridge was recently named one of the most dangerous in America. We prefer to think of it as vintage.

We have horse-drawn carriage tours downtown but it was Charleston that showed us how much nicer it is when the horses wear those diaper contraptions and we wish we'd thought of it first.

When I come back to my hometown from points south and cross that beautiful old bridge, I don't think about falling into the river below. I am way too busy falling in love all over again with Wilmington. It's the church spires that get me first; you can see them when you're still in Brunswick County. Closer to the bridge, you notice the gleaming twelve-story headquarters of a global pharmaceutical research organization anchoring the north end of the riverfront. To the south, the majestic cranes at the state port stand sentry over a fleet of tugboats and container ships from around the world.

Back at Rx, a hungry hodgepodge of film types, professors, and posers join a mix of grand old Wilmington families for Sunday brunch and bottomless mimosas, the former after a night of merrymaking; the latter after having sufficiently fattened the collection plate at "First Prez" and St. James Episcopal nearby.

So it was that I found myself, not fitting into any of those categories now that I think about it, enjoying a lovely breakfast and woefully eyeing the one biscuit the server placed in front of me. It was the size and color of a walnut.

"Can you see yourself clear to part with a few more of these?" I asked the server, who looked like I had slapped her in the face with a catfish. Locally sourced, of course.

While there's no doubt food tastes better, is fresher, and plates are lovelier at Wilmington's best restaurants today, I sometimes pine for the days of abundant portions.

See, it's still the South. And, in Wilmington, anyway, if we're really being honest about it, no manner of artsy makeover can take away our love for large quantities of good food. We remember, some of us, what it was like to order a plate of fried shrimp called a "barge" at Faircloth's on curvaceous Airlie Road. And, although it was technically at Wrightsville Beach, not Wilmington, we remember the Marina Restaurant, which had a Sunday buffet that offered exotic fare like Seafood Newburg AND had a nearly nekkid mermaid on the marquee. And we remember, the truly local among us, the hilariously fabulous New China Restaurant. It moved around a good bit and ended up on Oleander Drive before being demolished for alleged progress in the early 2000s. Only at a Chinese restaurant in Wilmington, North Carolina, would you be able to enjoy your meal in an intimate, curtained room, adorned with Chinese lanterns and silk drapes that didn't exactly go with the worn formica table and chairs. There, you could hear the very Southern waitress shuffle from one private dining room to the next, lean into the room, and holler: "Y'all want any more rolls and Pepsi with your chow mein?"

The Far East had met the Old South, and it was a beautiful marriage of good and plenty.

At the end of the day, when the sunsets on the river or salt marsh attain a shade of pink-gold that only filmmakers whose Kickstarter campaigns have done very well indeed seem to get just right, Wilmington's charm lies in its oddball blend of old and new, rural and urban, chic and casual.

It's why you will see the guests at a formal wedding here wearing a finely tailored suit (yes, from Charleston, *grrrr*) and shoes with no socks.

It's why you'll see a street preacher and his sidekicks, all heavily robed and standing on old lard tubs, preaching gospel just a few feet away from the city's "gentrified" Brooklyn Arts District, teeming with artists' studios, antique stores, and a beautiful old deconsecrated church that hosts everything from jazz concerts to high-end flea markets to weddings.

This is my home. It has always been my home. And as more and more of y'all discover it, I'm going to try and welcome you. Even if it kills me.

Celia Rivenbark
Summer 2015

CELIA RIVENBARK is the *New York Times* best-selling author of seven humor collections, a former Duke University media fellow, and a syndicated columnist for Tribune Media Services, whose work appears in newspapers across the country. The proudest moment of her life was when she earned enough from her first newspaper job to buy a washer and dryer and neither one of them had to go on the front porch. She lives in Wilmington with her husband, Scott Whisnant, and their daughter, Sophie.

A Place Called Home

Winter Beach Run

EMILY LOUISE SMITH

WINTER LIGHT SPARES NOTHING on this island. It lavishes equally the sailboats moored in Banks Channel, the boarded ice-cream stand on Lumina Avenue, the faded tank tops and towels in the display window of Wings. It bathes the egret in the salt marsh at the center of Harbor Island, where I begin my usual six-mile run, lingers on the boats shrink-wrapped and stacked four-high in dry docks, slides down metal awnings on the island's old cottages, which it clearly loves best. It pauses along the concrete face of St. Therese in the alcove over the Catholic church's sanctuary. This is Wrightsville Beach in the off-season, gloriously empty of tourists. If I time it right, I'll make it around the John Nesbitt Loop, out to the south end gazebo to stretch, just as the sun slips behind Masonboro Island like an orange coin down a jukebox's throat.

Some nights I run the beach end to end, four miles, without seeing another person. My favorite public accesses are the few sand paths left that cut through oleander and fig trees—those nestled between a rare undeveloped lot and old house. Wooden walls built to contain the dunes bulge with yucca and yaupon, wax myrtles and dwarf palmettos. The waves I can't hear when running along the marsh crescendo as I crest a walkway over the sand. No matter how many times I pass through here, the ocean is never less imposing. Everything's dialed up on this side: the smell of salt, the inky expanse of sky, the bright stories of constellations. "My god," I say to greet it, stretching my arms overhead, "I live here." There's no one to hear me. The rental houses are dark; the only conversation a few rooms that flicker on like code between condos. Come June, this section of beach is an obstacle course of chairs and coolers, children in tidal pools, sandcastles and moats. Summer leans close, and the humidity slows everything it touches, licks us sticky. But winter is clear and invigorating, makes my run fast and flat. Bitter winds from the northeast hustle clouds of loose sand down the beach that graze my skin like sandpaper. The wind grips my cheeks and eddies in my ears and head, my legs and lungs, as if the whole island were suddenly swirling in my chest. A good three miles in at this point, I exhale a laugh no one has ever heard—it's reserved for my romance with being alone.

My devotion to this winter beach run was hard won. I don't come naturally to Wilmington's soggy landscape, its rivers and marshes. For more than a decade now, the slippery place has left me feeling unsettled and exposed. Its barrier islands migrate with currents and wind; wandering inlets can close with a single storm. Friends buy boats, then lose them to the next hurricane. Mason's Inlet, which separates Wrightsville Beach from Figure Eight Island, has shifted more than a half mile south in the past fifteen years. Summer breezes push sand back to the northeast. Just look at the juniper trees to see how indecisive and twitchy the wind can be here, its ambivalence ensconced in their branches. When I first encountered the illustrations of Wilmington artist Claude Howell in the pages of Ben Dixon MacNeill's 1958 memoir, *The Hatterasman*, I couldn't explain how his sparse pen and ink drawings so deftly capture the spirit of the restless barrier islands. It would take me another five years of living here to fully appreciate what my friend and colleague Philip Gerard meant when he wrote that Howell's drawings are filled with wind.

While my mind has always craved room to move and experiment, my heart longs for cover. A native of the South Carolina Piedmont, I prefer the golden fanfare of ginkgo leaves, the Japanese maples that deepen in both spring and fall—colors that smell of smoke and hay. As kids, my sister and I tromped at the heels of our adventurous mother through the Appalachian forests of the Carolinas and Tennessee, scrambled across Grandfather Mountain's mile-high swinging bridge, and up craggy peaks to sweeping views of the valleys. Meanwhile our poor, acrophobic father was left clinging to a rock or a last, paltry stump before the mountaintop revealed itself. All these years later, though, it's not those summits, or the blanket of color spread beneath them, that have stayed with me, but rather the understory of mountain laurel and dogwood, light filtered through a canopy of oaks and eastern hemlocks, the coves of rhododendron that Dad loved. The old forest made me feel safe too. I relished wading across rocky creeks in outgrown Keds saved for this purpose, rejoiced when the counselors at summer camp led us into the woods and directed us to disburse with our notebooks, each to a separate trunk. The object was to lean back and simply observe: to record everything we saw, heard, and smelled—an exercise in reverie I've tried to replicate pretty much every day since.

Nearly two decades after moving away from the Piedmont, I can still pop a strawberry in my mouth, close my eyes, and taste back roads and farms, feel the unwashed brightness of the fruit give way to fields. "This is how you do it," my mother would say, demonstrating the perfect snap that eludes small, eager fingers, then open her fist to reveal the intact berry in her palm. It's one of my earliest, distinct memories: a crown of sun warming my head, juice staining my shirt and mouth. We counted the weeks until school started by which peach varietals filled the baskets at the stand: Monroe, Cresthaven, Loring. When I think of home, it's the trees and orchards I long for.

My first year living on the coast, I grieved that familiar pageant of color, the mountains and farm seasons that had taught me how to feel. Though the land my Scots-Irish great-grandparents tended wasn't mine to inherit, no longer belonged to us—if it ever did—I always belonged to it. So when

I left Wilmington after three years in graduate school to move back to South Carolina, I confess that I rather preferred the view of its downtown church steeples and antebellum columns awash in afternoon light, its grand riverboat *Henrietta*, framed in my rearview mirror. I couldn't have predicted that less than a year later, I'd drive back across the Cape Fear to accept a full-time teaching position at UNC Wilmington, and that, after more than a decade here, I'd still resist putting down roots. Don't get me wrong: I've built a rewarding career, a community of friends and fellow writers, helped found a magazine and my dream literary press, but I have not invested in a house, or even a condo. A house is a story that could go on for years, and some part of me needs to maintain the illusion that I might wander like an inlet.

34

I moved recently from a 1920s bungalow in Wilmington's historic Carolina Place—complete with a fireplace and creaking hardwood floors—to a house tucked along a prong of Bradley Creek. The marsh swells with moon tides, and every morning, even when the water is low, light floods the cordgrass. I miss the hundred-year-old live oaks that stood watch over those old houses, and I miss the neighbors who, as each house dispensed its last piece of Halloween candy, gathered on a single porch to outlast the final trick-or-treaters, drink beer, and tell stories. But now, I peer out my kitchen window to find a blue heron glide over the marsh, a nesting clapper rail. Once they herald spring, the peepers and other resident frogs don't give up their raucous chorus until late summer. I leave my porch light burning all night, because the bugs that accumulate around it occasionally draw the jewel-sized beauties out of the trees to my doorstep.

Across this coastal plain, vernal ponds ripen with barking frogs, Mabee's salamanders, and the fairy shrimp popularized as mail-order Sea-Monkeys. A few years ago, I bought a kayak to navigate the waterways of Harbor Island, and for several summers, paddled around the oyster beds and spartina, across the inlet to Masonboro Island. I learned the art of flipping my boat, pulling the spray skirt's cord, ejecting, and then scrambling back in. (A self-rescue known as a cowboy, it was easily my favorite trick.) But

I struggled to perfect the illusive roll, a skill essential to paddling ocean waves. Every week in January, including one when it snowed, I strapped my boat to the top of my Subaru and drove to the YMCA pool to practice submerging myself, sometimes twenty times an hour, until I was so exhausted and confused about the direction of the sky, a friend had to walk across the five-feet shallow end to right my boat and prevent me from drowning in panic. The object, she said, was just to hang upside down, not even release air from my nose, get comfortable underwater. But no matter how hard I tried, I couldn't relax. I could not convince myself there was the slightest thing natural about suspending oneself upside down in a kayak.

The sound of a waterfall is silence, the poet Jack Gilbert wrote. "The stillness I did not notice until the sound / of water falling made apparent the silence I had / been hearing long before." It never fails. I come home in September after a long day of teaching, push my key in the lock, and suddenly realize the frogs are gone and have taken summer with them. It's my new way of telling the seasons.

My proximity to the ocean now, this inching closer, is what makes beach runs possible several times a week. Outside the surf shop on the main corner, a camera holds the island's secrets like a diary and, on a monitor in the window, replays the feature: morning light dancing in the street outside Tower 7 (the fish taco restaurant I frequent for coffee and burritos after morning runs), the patient father whose children wag ice-cream painted tongues at it, the couple late at night, faces full of beer and fresh freckles, who can't contain the humidity and endless week in front of them without combusting in argument. I lengthen my stride, hold my head a little higher as I sail by the camera. If you could isolate the frames and shuffle them like a flipbook, you'd see a woman gradually shedding winter layers of smart wool, leggings, and gloves in favor of shorts and a tank top. You'd see my wind-chapped face become a pink, overripe berry in July, wet hair curl at the nape of my neck. You wouldn't notice a woman praying, her senses heightened, how acutely aware I am when I'm running. You wouldn't see me becoming a little more myself with each loop, the ideas I'm working out, or the paragraphs I'm writing. In a *New York Times* essay on running and writing, Joyce Carol Oates wrote, "On days when I can't run, I don't feel 'myself,' and whoever the self is I feel, I don't like nearly so much as the other." Maybe that's the paradox of stillness: Only when I'm in motion can I achieve the peace that allows me to see and hear clearly, to attune myself to my surroundings.

Though I've always relished the solitude of long, solo runs, I've also made some of my best friends in Wilmington while running this island. The beats of our feet, synced strides, and arms swinging in unison allow us to talk about love and loss, subjects that might not slip as easily from our mouths while sitting across from one another. Our late thirties and early forties have brought their share of hardships — cancer, miscarriage, divorce, rehab — but none of these has been off limits between us. Just as valuable, we've learned the increasingly rare gift of being quiet together. This winter, as we crossed the bridge, a close friend spotted a bottlenose dolphin in the channel. Like me, she confronts grief, not by retreating, but by turning up the speed and distance: endurance races, crack-of-dawn track workouts. It's one of many reasons we get along so well. We slowed to watch its dorsal fin windmill to the surface, vanish, and appear again. When it swam beyond sight, we picked up the pace again, but not the conversation. For a while, we ran in silence — simply held it, and everything unsaid but understood, between us.

The narrow barrier islands off Wilmington's coast are nesting grounds for loggerhead turtles, least terns, black skimmers, American oystercatchers, and piping plovers; and they serve as rest stops for thousands of migrating shorebirds. One August evening, while vacationing on a beach just south of here, I introduced myself to a pair of women wearing sun visors and matching turtle-watch T-shirts who had arranged their lawn chairs around the wire-mesh screen indicating a nest. The pot they were watching that night wasn't ready yet, but they must have sensed my eagerness and hastened me down the beach to another access — imploring my parents, sister, and brother-in-law to hurry it up, carrying a niece on piggyback — where for the first time we saw the sand boil, then a startlingly small two-inch turtle emerge on the surface. (Nothing like the three-hundred-pound rescued adults I'd witnessed at the aquarium.) By the time we arrived, twenty onlookers had gathered along a temporary shoot — families on after-dinner strolls, who, like us, would stumble on the most memorable night of their vacation. More aunts, grandparents, and neighbors were summoned until we formed a barefoot congregation.

It takes a long, wondrous hour for 114 turtles to clumsily parade, flipper over flipper, to the sea, but not nearly as long for me to fall in love with this odd but equitable arrangement, this impromptu cluster of humans. Previously unknown to each other, we stood shoulder-to-shoulder from the dune's edge to the sea, united in deflecting ghost crabs and raccoons. We'd silently agreed: We will at least get them this far safely.

My photos of the night are blurs of blue. Flashes weren't allowed, as the light could confuse the hatchlings that still had a twenty-hour swim ahead of them, another round of predators they'd have to survive on their own. As light faded from the day, a volunteer raised a lantern to imitate the moon.

Maybe home is an idea that can lie dormant in us for a long time before it rises and floods us with familiarity. Like the fairy shrimp eggs, waiting years in the loamy soil for a good spring rain to become a vernal pond and coax them to life. Or the peepers that survive winter beneath a loose shingle of bark, nearly icicles, except for the antifreeze fluids slowly coursing through their veins. Which brings me to another summer night I keep tucked in my memory. As I rounded the corner near the athletic fields that border the parking lot, a toy airplane whirred by, dragging the pink banner of sunset in behind it. I lingered there, stretching, as more enthusiasts arrived and spaced out across the field, each attached to a miniature aircraft. The oncoming dark buzzed with planes diving and wheeling over-head like illuminated sea birds. Spectators gathered, and I leaned close to watch a father wrap his son's arms, their four hands guide the remote that, for a little while at least, tethered our hearts to the sky.

EMILY LOUISE SMITH is the publisher of *Ecotone* magazine and Lookout Books, a liter-ary imprint she co-founded in 2009. She teaches in the creative writing department at UNC Wilmington, where she also directs the publishing certificate program. Her honors include fellowships from the Studios of Key West, Hambidge, and the Hub City Writers Project, as well as a Dorothy Sargent Rosenberg Prize. Her poems and essays appear in *Best New Poets*, the *Southern Review*, *New South*, and *Literary Publishing in the 21st Century*.

The Greens on Queen

RHONDA BELLAMY

EVERYONE KNEW THE GREENS on Queen Street, four sisters all nestled in the 600 block. My Grandmother Bell, former personal aide to the legendary entertainer Peg Leg Bates, lived with her sister Helen. Helen ran the elevator in the Murchison Building. Three doors down, their younger sister Ann, a born caregiver, lived in the house directly across from their oldest sister, Mary, who had just returned to Wilmington after years of living in Harlem, New York.

By the time Mary traded her 119th Street brownstone for the modest wood-frame house on Queen Street, she had perfected the art of the party: food to feed an army, free flowing spirits, and family.

In addition to the Green sisters, every other home on Queen Street was inhabited by cousins or lifelong friends who volleyed the day's news in whispered shouts over the cobbled street. Passersby would pause to chat, one foot hoisted on a porch step, as they added to the daily digest of local happenings before making their way up or down the street.

It was 1976 and I was newly arrived in Wilmington myself. My parents had tired of New York City's frenzy and wanted to come back Down South with me and my siblings in tow. For months leading up to the move, our parents regaled us with memories of their hometown. "W-Town," as they called it, was a mystical place where you could leave your front door open, and sleep on the porch, and have cookouts in your own backyard.

The Greens, my father's large maternal family, needed no excuse to throw a party and the extended circle of friends needed no invitation. My Great-aunt Mary might have been Mary Clingman of Harlem, New Yawk, but in her backyard on Queen Street, she was simply Tit.

For the sisters the festivities began the day before. One sister would pry open frozen clams with a butter knife to scoop out the makings of the family-favorite fritters. This one chopped onions; that one bell peppers; another whipped up the batter. There was lively banter between the sisters and others who knew the *eve* of the cookout was every bit as entertaining.

"Who the hell invited you?" Tit would randomly ask—her version of a warm welcome.

By the next morning, a motley mix of kitchen chairs and metal porch furniture was gathered from the sisters' houses so everyone could have a seat around the card tables and fish fryers.

We teenagers naturally picked a remote part of the backyard, where we would go to mimic the sisters who all had a thing about screen doors and who were always armed with newspaper swatters.

"Don't let the screen door slam! Shut that screen door! You just let a fly in!"

After we tired of our mimicry and other teen talk, we'd wander back to the fryers to wait for our fish or fritter to come out.

"Junior, tell them about the time that Maxine . . ." Tit would prompt my father. And he'd recount one of his younger sister's many antics, which always drew hearty laughter from the growing circle of family and friends.

Throughout the day, my father would alternate between animated story-telling and leading the family in song. There was always music:

People all over the world, join hands
Start a love train, love train

or

It's so nice to see
All the folks you love together
Sittin' and talkin' 'bout
All the things that's been goin' down
It's been a long, long time
Since we had a chance to get together
Nobody knows the next time we see each other
Maybe years and years from now
Family reunion (Got to have)
A family reunion
Family reunion
(It's so nice to come together) To come together
(To get together)

The O'Jays provided the anthems for the Queen Street gatherings. Even the flies flitted in harmony.

In stages we would all migrate to the other sisters' porches, where we happened upon new visitors and old memories.

"Remember when your daddy brought you down here with him," Aunt Helen said to me. "You cried from the time you hit town until the time you left."

In fact it was my first memory of Queen Street. I was about four years old and had accompanied my father "home" for a short visit. I remember a small cot in a dimly lit room and an insufferable smell I would later come to know as kerosene.

Queen Street was the landing for the far-flung. It was the place you checked into upon arrival in Wilmington and checked out of upon departure. It was where the New York branch of the family tree packed their chicken sandwiches, and brown dogs, and cheap cigarettes before heading back up I-95.

Back at the cookout, more people have arrived and others are beginning the progressive porch visits we've just completed. Aluminum-foil–covered styrofoam plates of fried fish, clam fritters, potato salad, and greens glint in the summer sun. Back and forth all day.

It is night. Tit has long since dispensed of shoes, teeth, and decorum. She is holding court in the midst of all she holds dear. Sisters and nieces and nephews and neighbors. It is apparent that she feels no pain when, in her inimitable ribald fashion, she loudly proclaims to the large group of family and friends, "Get the hell out!"

And we all laugh—because we *are* out.

We are on Queen Street in "W-town" where you can leave your front door open, and sleep on the porch, and have cookouts in your own backyard.

We're home.

RHONDA BELLAMY is executive director of the Arts Council of Wilmington and New Hanover County. A veteran journalist, she is former news director of a five-station radio consortium, on which she hosted a daily talk show, "On the Waveline with Rhonda Bellamy." She has written and edited three books: *Moving Forward Together: A Community Remembers 1898*, *My Restless Journey* (the memoirs of iconic community leader Bertha Boykin Todd), and *Meet the Help: An Anthology of True Stories*, inspired by the best-selling novel *The Help*.

Restorations

GWENYFAR

"When is our anniversary?"

"August 25."

"I haven't missed it?"

"No, you still have time."

"Okay, don't tell your father I can't remember."

"You know, I would just like to point out that I am the only person in this equation who was not present for the marriage."

"I know that, dear. You remind me every year."

Then my mother would hang up, and a couple of days later, my father would call and ask me the same questions. These conversations would begin in May and continue until mid-August, when I would remind both of them of the need to make dinner reservations for their upcoming special occasion on August 25.

Even after my mother passed away, my father continued asking about their anniversary. It was as if somehow he could just remember it, he could grab hold of it like a talisman.

Buying presents for my parents was like breathing underwater. My mother hated almost everything that was ever given to her, and my father didn't pay enough attention to the world to notice presents that were not ingestible. Knowing this, I began in my early twenties to commemorate their important events with experiences (trips or concert tickets, for example) or practical matters like home repairs. To acknowledge one occasion, I decided to restore the playhouse in my parents' backyard.

Scratch the image in your head. I'm not talking about a simple plywood structure or a tiny lean-to or even a plastic playhouse from the Eighties. I grew up in a historic mansion that was right out of a novel. Sometime around the turn of the twentieth century, a fire took out the first house on the property, but the playhouse survived. My playhouse, over one hundred years old, had been around longer than our rambling mansion.

The playhouse was built with glass windows that opened and closed and an Alice in Wonderland door with a real lockset and skeleton key unlike anything that can be found in the door aisle at Lowe's.

I discovered the playhouse one Saturday afternoon while hacking away at the vines and thorns that had taken over the yard. The family that built the house had let it decay around them after their matriarch passed away. As I was tearing through the tangled jungle, a white structure began to materialize in front of me. When I saw my seven-year-old reflection in one of the tiny windows, I felt like I'd just stepped into a fairytale.

During my childhood, the big house consumed most of our family's attention. But I did get to pick out a lovely sky-blue paint color for the playhouse and spend a weekend with Mommy priming and painting the interior. At five-foot-three my mother could just barely stand up in the center of the cathedral ceiling. We then hung filmy white curtains on the windows. I was disappointed that Mommy was not willing to invest in shades since the hardware was there for hanging them.

Perhaps most surprising all those years later was that it was already decorated when I found it under all the overgrown vines and brambles:

Framed pictures hung on the walls; an antique rattan-weave chair, a folding table, and two metal chairs were in place as though a tea party was about to begin.

We were only the second family to live in the grand house. It had been built by the Hooper family (descendants of the signer of the Declaration of Independence). Even as a child, I had a sense that the playhouse missed the Hooper children and their friends. But now after decades of neglect it seemed to be welcoming me back.

I remember burying treasure under the steppingstones leading to the playhouse porch. It was shocking to discover back then that dirt could get into my buried pirate chests. Mommy suggested zip-lock sandwich baggies. "But pirates didn't use those!" I protested. There was absolutely no mention of zip-lock baggies anywhere in *Treasure Island*.

"They probably would have if they had been available," she reasoned.

I shook my head *no* in frustration.

"Look, it's up to you. But do you want your treasure maps and buried treasure to be destroyed by rain and mud?"

After the next rainstorm I snuck into the kitchen and pocketed several baggies. Somehow it seemed very un-pirate-like to ask my mom for them.

That little house became the space I brought my toys, my friends, and especially my beagle, Coppy. Mommy would bring lunch straight to the front door, and on weekends, she and Daddy would stay in the backyard with me until the sun went down. The playhouse was the center of our universe, although we never got around to fixing it up properly with a new roof and replacing the slowly rotting siding.

When friends would come over they could not believe how incredible my little house was. Even as teenagers, my friends and I liked to hang out in it, even though we had to crouch under the low ceiling. We would feel very grown up and have retro days, scrunched into my child-sized furniture. I remember wondering if any future generations of children would play there after me.

I went away to college, and the playhouse hosted another occupant — my dog, Coppy. Though he had a doghouse, Coppy decided the playhouse was much nicer and moved in. After he died, the playhouse became a storage shed, with garden hoses, chicken wire, shovels, and other shed-like items wedged between the furniture and pictures, a sort of miniature Grey Gardens — a shabby, decaying version of its former glory.

Decades later, I scraped down the little house's exterior, intending to paint and surprise my parents for Christmas. But the scraping uncovered considerably more decay than expected. I began calling carpenters, asking for estimates on restoration. "It's actually built like a real house — down to the piers and the plaster walls!" one carpenter exclaimed. Everyone who saw it was surprised by the level of detail and care that had been involved in its construction, but they hemmed and hawed when it came to pricing or committing to the job. One carpenter took on the job of repairing the door, but returned it without its beautiful, historic lockset. Years later, I am still livid. The playhouse isn't complete without the skeleton key.

Then in 2009, my friend Eric agreed to restore it, promising to finish it in time for my parents' August anniversary. But my mother died unexpectedly. The restoration was no longer a priority. Frankly, I wasn't emotionally up to it right then.

A few years later, I was ready, and my childhood friend Jeremy, who was working as a carpenter, agreed to take on the project. Over those few years, however, the playhouse had once again been reclaimed by Mother Nature. In the midst of his own trying time, Jeremy joined me in taming this otherworldly place, framed by seven-foot-high azaleas. Wisteria wound around us, and as we hacked and pulled, our troubles fell away. Jeremy heedfully fitted new wood, milled to match the playhouse's original siding. He replaced the low-vaulted ceiling. Just as carefully, we forged a new future without the people we were missing — the people whose losses we felt so profoundly. Jeremy's recently departed brother, Josh, and my mother—neither of us could have ever prepared for or imagined a future without them. Lucas, Jeremy's eight-year-old son, danced around the yard helping his dad, listening to stories about us as children—a time he could only imagine as a hundred years ago.

"No, that's when the playhouse was built," I chided. "Your dad and I are only thirty years old." But to an eight-year-old, a century and a third of a century are both far, far away.

"Do you want me to rebuild the mantel?" Jeremy asked, outlining the ghostmarks on the wall where the mantelpiece had been ripped away more than fifty years earlier. I started to decline. It hadn't been there in my childhood when he and I had played there. But I was struck by the fact that this wasn't about bringing it back to my memories. It was about making the house whole again. "Yes, that would be really nice . . . Thanks for suggesting it." Jeremy worked to finish the project in time for me to present it to my then-ailing father for Father's Day that June.

The only task left to do was to paint. I began it, but the demands on my time, especially with caring for my dad, made it impossible. So I hired a young man, who made great show of taping windows and arranging tools but did very little painting.

History reared her ugly head and again my plans for the big unveiling were derailed by loss.

My father passed away in May, before Father's Day and before the playhouse was finished.

Eventually, my special haven in the yard was made structurally and cosmetically sound, painted both inside and out.

It seems odd to me that our family managed to fully renovate our three-story home twice in twenty years, but it took a quarter of a century to restore a one-room playhouse. I can still hear the very serious conversations of my tea parties with Coppy and the dolls wafting out the windows. Though small in scope, this singular enduring structure is grander to me than any white-columned mansion. Its four walls have witnessed more elation and excitement than any other walls I know.

For the first time in decades, I haven't had anyone ask me if they had missed their anniversary yet. Instead, on August 25, I mix together the two boxes of my parents' ashes and scatter them around the playhouse, where I hope they will mingle for all eternity with the echoes of my childhood laughter.

GWENYFAR is proud to manage her family's independent bookstore, Old Books on Front St., in Wilmington. She is a theater reviewer for *Encore Magazine* and routinely fails to recognize the famous when they visit the bookstore. She considers herself the luckiest person on the planet to have shared her adult life with Jock Brandis, humanitarian and inventor, though he has occasionally ended up as a figure of humor in her writing. They have two dogs, Horace and Hilda Rumpole.

Where You Find It

MELODIE HOMER

WILMINGTON LIES BETWEEN the Atlantic Ocean and Cape Fear River. Its beaches are shared by surfers, fishermen, joggers, and families with children playing in the waves. Anyone who wants to read, walk the beach, or watch the waves feels the salty, warm breezes and peacefulness the ocean brings. In the historic downtown, the riverfront is home to many local musicians and artists who showcase their creations at the frequent street fairs and craft shows.

Wilmington is a city with a few subtle contradictions. College students, empty nesters, and young families share this beachside haven with the first of the baby-boomer retirees. Northerners also flood Wilmington, since it sits at the halfway point between New York and Florida. It's a place that seems to seduce travelers, where they waver and often decide to make Wilmington their final destination. This is the story for many, different versions of how Wilmington came to be home.

My story begins with an ending, a devastating loss that left my young children with only one parent and me without a spouse. Tuesday, September 11, 2001, my husband LeRoy was killed. He had been at work, co-piloting United Airlines Flight 93 when his plane was hijacked, the fourth of that morning, the biggest terrorist act on American soil. This flight would eventually become known as the flight of heroes, as the plane did not reach its destination: the U.S. Capitol, where a bronze plaque recognizes each crewmember and passenger for saving the lives of many in Washington, DC.

For years after that day, my life felt like it was vacillating between infamy and then, as time went by, apathy. I was proud of my husband, yet I didn't want to be labeled a 9/11 widow, to be defined by the worst day of my life. I felt stuck, unable to move forward, with my entire community looking to me every time an anniversary came around. A decade after LeRoy's death, I felt like I had survived those ten years without living them. I realized if I wanted to find my way back to contentment, perhaps a similar version of what I had shared with LeRoy, I would have to look for it.

I had always dreamed of living close to the ocean.

> At the beach, life is different. Time doesn't move hour to hour but mood to moment. We live by the currents, plan by the tides, and follow the sun. —*Author unknown*

My family needed the slow rhythm and healing power of the ocean's beauty, its sounds and smells, the warmth of the sun. I noticed all these things on my first visit to Wilmington. And now we're here and it feels different than any other place I've lived. At first it's almost imperceptible. Traffic moves slower; there's an absence of car horns. Wilmingtonians smile, stop, and hold doors. The patience with which people interact with each other is caring and considerate.

No sooner had we moved in than I was impressed with the kind gestures of our new neighbors. Entire families appeared at our door to introduce themselves, bring baked goods, flowers, and cards announcing each family member, and graciously provide contact information for any help we might need.

It's been a good move, but there are still mornings when the feelings of sadness, of being overwhelmed, almost keep me in bed. Then I look out the window and the sun convinces me to start my day. I walk outside, and the first or second person I encounter greets me with a smile, or asks me how my day is going. My favorite coffee shop knows my name and what I want to order. I often run into a neighbor there and we stop for a minute and catch up. Soon, I am feeling like myself.

All over town—at the beach, in the grocery store, at a restaurant—during the course of the day, I might run into one of my children's old teachers, my daughter's horseback riding instructor, and friends from the gym. In a city of 100,000 people, the degrees of separation seem few. Since we moved here, a community has formed around me and my children. I have developed close friendships with neighbors, co-workers, church members. My children made friends our first day here. Invitations were extended when meeting someone for the first time that led to new friendships.

I remember one of my first experiences in Wilmington. We were having Thanksgiving dinner at the Pilot House on the Cape Fear River. My son started to have a tantrum because he had not eaten his meal and I was not allowing him to have dessert. While I quickly tried to get the check and pack up his dinner for later, I was embarrassed by how loud he became as other patrons were trying to enjoy a nice holiday meal. Then I noticed an older woman making her way over to our table. She sat down with us and asked my son what was the matter. She talked to him quietly, patiently, until he calmed down. I asked her if she was a teacher. "No, just a mom."

I could not believe a stranger had been so empathetic when she saw I was struggling. I heard no negative comments about my son from anyone dining that night. The kindness of that stranger, and in fact all the diners there, has stayed with me for years. It would be the first of many times that a stranger would help me. Random acts of kindness are the norm here.

Wilmington has a personality, which is as much about mild temperatures, breathtaking sunsets, and water views that surround you as go about your day. That beauty and the kindness of the people who live here are what make it feel like home. Unexpectedly you start to feel like you are part of Wilmington. This feeling creeps in slowly, almost like falling in love. It changes you, softens you, and then you realize that the beauty of this place is, above all, its people.

That's the way I would describe my Wilmington. I find I have become kinder and more patient. I worry less and laugh more. I relax more than I have in a long while. I have already made lifetime friends here. I look forward to what is ahead for me and my family. This is where we were meant to be.

MELODIE HOMER has been a registered nurse for over twenty years and works as a clinical instructor. She is the founder and president of the LeRoy W. Homer Jr. Foundation since its inception in 2002. This nonprofit organization helps young men and women take their first step in aviation careers by awarding flight scholarships to obtain private pilot certification. She is the author of *From Where I Stand: Flight #93 Widow Sets the Record Straight.* She lives in Wilmington with her two children, their dog, and many new friends.

Ode to My Backyard

ROBERT ANTHONY SIEGEL

THE FOUR OF US stood back to admire our handiwork: eight spindly tomato plants tied to stakes pushed into the ground. With the kale and the peas to the left, and the carrots and basil to the right, the little corner of our backyard that we'd marked off for a garden was full. My wife and I hugged; the kids cheered.

We were transplants, just like those tomatoes. Six months earlier we had moved to North Carolina from New York City, where we'd lived in an apartment ten stories above the West Side Highway. Our backyard had been the dingy brown hall that led between the garbage chute and the elevator; that's where we ran our children on days it was too wet to get to the park.

And here we were now, standing in an earthly paradise, a little bewildered by this kind of happiness. It wasn't an unusually large backyard, no bigger than our neighbors', but it seemed vast. The air around us was busy with big fat bees and butterflies of a strange flittery green. An enormous, brawny pecan tree rose behind us, and droopy or bushy flowering things ran along the fence: camellias, azaleas, roses, lilies, lantana, wisteria, jasmine—we were still learning the names. In the center of it all rose a magnificent pine tree, taller than our house.

The next weeks were busy, but now and then I would kneel beside the tomato plants, amazed first by the hard green knobs that had sprouted among the leaves, and then by the way those knobs began to fill out and take on that familiar tomato shape I knew from the supermarket, to grow red and soft. This might actually work, I thought, realizing for the first time that I hadn't expected it to, that I had assumed the plants would wither and my family and I would get in the car and speed back to New York, where life would resume its familiar, safe shape.

A part of me *wanted* to get in the car and step on the gas. Living close to the land had a worrisome side. My daughter had found a snake by the azalea bush and I had pulled everyone inside for a week, till I worked up the nerve to put on a pair of hip-waders, grab a baseball bat, and go searching for it.

And then there was the human element. The kindly old neighbor to our left had stopped me at the fence one morning to suggest that I cut down the pine tree. "Don't you see which way it's leaning? In a storm it'll fall down right smack on my garage." He gave me a sweet smile. "It's for your own protection, son. I'd be heartbroken if I had to sue you."

I looked at the tree, which was straight, so thick I couldn't get my arms around it, and wondered what the local etiquette was in this kind of situation. Not knowing, I fell back on the New York version. "Of course, I'll counter sue."

"Son, you just lost the best neighbor you ever had."

Those were the last words he spoke to us. From then on he just glared across the fence, and when he wasn't there to glare, he left his hounds outside to bark.

I brooded about all of this, of course, because all of it seemed to have some mysterious bearing on whether we would survive in this strange new land. Seated on the front porch one night, I was so busy brooding that I almost missed the possum heading into the backyard. It was fat and

54

squat, with an elderly bald head, big shining eyes, and a dirty leer like a men's room flasher—the wet smile of a creature up to some great, illicit pleasure. He seemed to be panting with the effort of making his short legs go. I watched him disappear into the darkness, horrified.

I slept badly that night. The sound of the bullfrogs was deafening and the sheer darkness through our windows felt awful and wrong. Night in New York was full of light from streetlamps and office buildings, but this darkness was black enough to hide snakes and possums. I waited till dawn, stepped around the spider web, and went out to look at the garden. And that's when I saw that someone had taken a single juicy bite out of each and every one of our tomatoes. The sense of violation was terrible. They looked like human bites, and I knew instantly that it was our neighbor, exacting his revenge. I also knew what I was going to do about it: kill his dogs.

My wife trooped out with the kids to take a look. "It must be that possum," she said.

"Hey, look," said my son, pointing up at the pine tree.

A bird as big as a child was perched in one of the topmost branches. "A blue heron," I whispered, too awed to raise my voice. "Just like in the bird book." It had a long neck and hunched shoulders and a fiercely intelligent face reminiscent of my grandfather. We watched as it took flight, heading to the creek beyond our yard. My wife and I hugged; the kids cheered.

ROBERT ANTHONY SIEGEL is the author of two novels, *All the Money in the World* and *All Will Be Revealed.* His work has appeared in numerous venues, including the *New York Times,* the *Los Angeles Times,* the *Oxford American, Tablet, Tin House, Ploughshares, Bookforum,* and the *Los Angeles Review of Books.* He has been recognized with O. Henry and Pushcart Prizes, among other awards. His website is www.robertanthonysiegel.com.

Close-Ups

Pine Straw & the Ocean

JASON MOTT

IT WAS 3 A.M. AND COLD OUTSIDE and there we were groping one another in the backseat of a car in Hugh MacRae Park. It was my first time but I didn't have the heart to tell her that, on account of how she had warned me, more than once, that the last thing she wanted was to have someone fall in love with her. She had just finished trying her hand at love and all it had done was treat her badly—she was always vague about the definition of *badly* and I could never find the courage to ask for clarification. So, because I knew it was what she wanted to hear, I told her that I wouldn't fall in love with her and that she was not my first and that, when we had committed the act at hand, I would be able to let her go.

I won't say for certain that she believed my lie but she told me she did.

So I lost my virginity in Hugh MacRae Park at 3 a.m. in the backseat of a weary old Honda and even though it was cold outside we cracked the windows and the smell of pine needles and the ocean filled the car and when it was over I drove her home and she kissed me goodbye and smiled and told me, "You're cute."

We broke up six months later on account of how the guy she had once loved who had treated her *badly* called her one day out of the blue and promised her he had changed and that everything would be different this next time around and so, all of a sudden, I found myself in Hugh MacRae Park again at 3 a.m. and, this time, I was being told that everything was coming to an end between us:

EXT. HUGH MACRAE PARK. NIGHT.

A parked car sits in a deserted parking lot. Inside the car, two figures — MAN: early twenties, average build; WOMAN: midtwenties, thin, beautiful. Traffic hums in the distance.

WOMAN

I just can't walk away if he's really going to try.

MAN

You said that all you wanted was to get away from him.

WOMAN

I love him.

MAN

What about me?

WOMAN

I warned you.

END

When I took her home that night she hugged me goodbye before getting out of the car and we both promised to stay in touch and we both promised that, after an appropriate amount of time, maybe we would try our hand at friendship. Then she kissed me and left and I never saw her again.

Last I heard she had moved away from Wilmington. Whether the man who had treated her badly went with her is anybody's guess. I've never been able to decide which would be easier: the thought that he had truly changed and that she was with him and happy, or the thought that everything had gone wrong between them and that she needed to move just to get away from the memories.

Years later I would find myself in another part of Wilmington with another woman I would fall in love with in spite of her warnings and we would sit on her porch in early autumn talking of poetry with a group of friends and, after a little while, she would send everyone else away and ask me to linger and we would get up after a few hours—just as the sun was about to break over Wrightsville Beach—and she would lead me into the antebellum home that she rented and into her bedroom and I would fall in love with her just the way I had fallen in love with the woman in Hugh MacRae Park and she would never love me back just like that other woman and, as I left her apartment the next day, the smell of pine straw and the ocean would come rushing back to me and I would head back to Hugh MacRae Park and park my car and sit there with the windows down and cry and pretend that I did not know the reason for it.

Eventually, this second woman would move away as well.

I won't live in Wilmington forever. And, even if I did, there will come a day when Hugh MacRae Park is not there—removed by bulldozer or hurricane or simply the forward, indelible march of development. A time will come when I cannot go back there again, when I cannot sit in my car with the windows down on a summer night and remember things as I wished they had been rather than the way they actually were.

But, in the interim, the earth turns and the stars shine and the park still exists and on the right nights I can go there and walk and the pine straw and beach sand still smell like a twice-broken heart. But they also smell like love given freely, which is all love has ever been.

JASON MOTT is a best-selling author of two novels, *The Wonder of All Things* and *The Returned,* and two poetry collections. He received both his BFA and MFA degrees from the University of North Carolina at Wilmington. He currently lives in Bolton, North Carolina.

Dog & Wolf

The Time Between
(essay as ideolocator)

HANNAH DELA CRUZ ABRAMS

1.

THEY SLEPT WITH the engagement ring under the bed for three years. He proposed, she wavered, and the whole business was shoved into a gray lockbox under the bed, where only the cat would visit it.

2.

Aquae et ignis communiciationem. The sharing of fire and water. The phrase was used in the marriage vows of Ancient Rome. I feel uneasy, thinking about it. The elements themselves seem to be warning us off. Besides, I keep confusing it with *aquae et ignis interdiction*—banishment.

Banishment, I say out loud to the dog.

He looks back at me.

I am trying to decide if the word is lovely in its sound.

Banishment, I tell him again. It has a music I like. But then, I am not qualifying or applying it.

The night is unusually quiet. At the end of the dark avenue, a streetlamp has been replaced and the sweetgum blazes miraculous and verdant in the new glow. The dog is sleeping again, and his dream is troubled. His legs move and he sucks his teeth. He growls and whimpers.

Banishment, I whisper to wake him. I guess the music changes depending on the questions *To?* and *From what?*

3.

Lately, I have felt myself to be in a state of between.

The thought returned, out on the water with an old friend. An osprey hovered above us as we moved through a marsh, our paddles dripping. My friend saw it first, pointed up, and we watched its easing ecliptics. Almost, the bird seemed to stop and hover. In its talons, a silver flounder.

I have been examining myself for signs of loneliness and coming up short. The moments are still there, but nothing sustained. Mainly, I detect relief and a fledgling detachment. Also, a lump in my throat. When I think of the relief, apprehension chases smugness through me in a merry game. The lump goes unacknowledged even if, looking back later, it is there.

This is the first summer in ages that I have been well enough to enter the world. One thing about sickness, it teaches a body to be alone.

At any rate, I already need to revise: I have re-entered the world, but not all the way. Hence the betweenity.

The hawk dropped silently into the marsh, out of view. Our paddles cut the shallow water, disturbing the skate and silt beneath. In summer, the channel has an aquatic denseness, the depth muddy and opaque, but winter will usher in a cloudless sound. I will be able to follow, prone on my board, the tracks of herons and egrets, fine and precise as pencil sketches under the rushing tide.

You can be between a lot of things. I looked them up. Some of the things are:

wind and water
a rock and a hard place
decks
the moon and New York City

But also, and this is where I feel like I am approaching an answer:

between lights
between whiles
between you and me
between ourselves

Let us say then that this essay is an accounting of dusk as I am currently experiencing it.

between two lights
between my selves

4.

Across town, we laughed about the ring. We shook our heads over it. *What a mess*, some of us said. I told them what I knew: that this guy bought a ring when he wasn't dating anyone. He only knew he wanted to be married one day, so when his dad called from Jersey to say how a buddy—a jeweler—was dying of cancer and unloading his store cheap to pay for chemo, this guy jumped and got a ring that no one would see until it re-emerged from the lockbox, during a second proposal, when his fiancée finally held out a nervous finger.

They had been sleeping so long by then with one future pent-up, holding its breath and waiting, under the bed. I don't know if they mentioned it to each other before sleep, or if she sometimes took it out and looked at it before putting it back.

I gave in, she said. She laughed a little at the admission, and picked up a ribbon with which to tease my cat. Through the diamond-paned window, I could see a light wind move the camellias until they shrugged, pink and hopeful.

That was a long time ago, before I got sick. Back when every part of me was hungering, desirous, toe-tapping. I was a teenager when I met the man I've loved for half my life. He had a lopsided smile, benthic eyes, and an oceanic amble that stopped me short.

Our first night together, we drove down to Holden Beach, ate blackened tuna sandwiches on a floating dock hung with string lights, and talked about atoms and cosmic dust. We went to the empty beach and drank the bottle of warm, red wine pulled from the trunk of his old VW, and swam out into a lightning storm.

He said, *I could hold you.*

I said, *Yes.*

I have never seen it since on this coast, but we had a bioluminescent sea. The light lived in blue sparks on the tips of waves and in white sheets flashing on the horizon. We rose and fell, my hair catching in his teeth, the sharp blade of his shoulder clipping my chin, our feet never touching the bottom.

It's true that we laughed, my friends and I, over the story of the ring, but in what moment are any of us not giving in to one future over another.

5.

Entre chien et loup. In half-light, it's hard to determine if the shape loping through the woods is dog or wolf. And isn't all romance an imperfectly illuminated landscape? Certainly I have never been able to tell from danger.

I love to watch the fine mist of the night come on, The windows and the stars illumined, one by one. This from Baudelaire, who knew something about uncertainty.

I have always been partial to the in-betweens.

Every few years, I re-encounter the man I love, and the air goes electric. After we swam in the summer storm, he drove me to his family's

65

beach house. The roads were empty and hot, and we went speeding over them in full summer fashion, slipping on the bends from one lane to another, the speakers buzzing with volume, each of us with a hand out of the window cutting the wind.

There were lighthouses everywhere in that echoing beach house — miniature lighthouses, photographs of lighthouses.

He ran his hand up my sea-dampened skirt in the kitchen. In a marble bathroom, he played for me a beautiful guitar.

Better acoustics, he had said, pulling me by the hand into the room. We sat for hours in a monumental bathtub. He was shirtless, his jeans bleached and sandy. I put my pruny feet on top of his. The candlelight leapt into the hollows of his cheeks. We have spent many incomplete nights together since, but this was the closest we ever came to each other.

To this day, I can look back over the expanse of years, and he will notice my gaze, glance up, and the music returns just like that — it expands, rises.

Some hours before dawn, he showed me two rooms. You can sleep here, with me, he said, or you can take that room over there.

I gestured shyly to the guestroom and chose one future over another.

Well, our meetings are separated by more and more time. We work wider circles, and I am waiting for the time that the line between us breaks completely and unfurls in some other direction, at which point there will be no way to determine how long he has already been gone.

She loved me, sometimes I loved her too, supplies Neruda.

Once, he broke lemon verbena on my wrist and my skin carried the scent for days.

Once, he chased me down a long garden and around a sapling and when we at last went in, he waved up at the evening sky and said, *Goodnight, Mr. Moon.*

Once, in a doorframe, he kissed me with his hands on my waist. I said, *You're pushing and pulling at me.*

He said, *I know.*

He said, *After I communicate with you I feel as if I am disobeying God in the time between.*

Well, that gave me pause.

I love you as certain dark things are to be loved, in secret, between the shadow and the soul. Neruda, nudging.

6.

Here is a kind of night: I was sick. For some hours I was given a terminal diagnosis. The sheets were sweat-dampened, and dishes piled up in the sink. Bees and flies gathered dust on the windowsills. It was a night that lasted two years and it was empty of sound. On holidays, the phone didn't ring, but the silence did.

If I could catch the feeling, I would: the feeling of the singing of the real world, as one is driven by loneliness and silence from the habitable world. Woolf set this down in her diary.

I didn't catch the feeling either, but my eyes adjusted to the dark, my ears to the silence, and when I came back to the habitable world, I found that it sang too loudly.

7.

Not to be outdone by the spectacle of the once lock-boxed ring, the wedding invitations showed up as messages in bottles. The bottles were large and plastic and damaged by travel. It was necessary to retrieve them from the parcel windows of the post office. The messages were impossible to extricate. Some of us got impatient and went at the contraptions with knives and gritted teeth until we were left standing, panting, in tiny piles of sand and gripping tiny scrolls.

One of the oldest messages in a bottle to turn up had drifted in the North Sea for nearly ninety-eight years before being hoisted aboard by a Scotsman on the ship *Copious.* In nearly a century, the bottle had traveled only ten miles. It came onto the trawler as by-catch in a haul of haddock and cod and monkfish. Six years earlier, a different skipper found another of oldest messages in a bottle. He was, strangely and poetically, also sailing on *Copious.*

There is, I am learning, another message in a bottle now in the running for the oldest on record. It was found in Tofino and appears to be dated 1906, which predates the other by eight years.

I am trying to summon up, about these discoveries, a trace of awe, but there is instead only a faint sense of disappointment that nothing more ancient has been retrieved from a bottle in the sea. As a child, I threw them in regularly but neglected to include contact information, so I will never hear back. Perhaps bottle-throwers in general, though, are little entitled to answers.

My guess is that the irony was lost on the bride and groom. When the wedding invitations were selected, my guess is that the betrothed were hoping to produce a trace of awe.

The truth is that most messages were hurled into the sea to discover drift and current. To see the movement of the world. To understand the future.

Or, to keep tabs on an enemy whose course and conviction are unknown.

8.

Entre in French is also the conjugated present tense of *Entrer*, to enter. I have begun to see *entre chien et loup* as "enter dog and wolf," which is a bit like the opposite of being between them. I like this as an option, the combination of safety and danger.

Some might argue that in terms of light, though, nothing changes. Between light and dark. Enter light and dark. With light, there are only degrees of lessening light.

Even in the trench, near my birthplace in the Mariana Islands, which is the deepest point on earth and where no sunlight reaches, bioluminescence flares. In absolute dark, we make our own light.

9.

Here is another kind of night: In my early twenties, I entered it. I pulled into the driveway, got out, turned the knob. It was the darkest night I ever saw. The hallway was night and the kitchen was night and the living room was night and the striped beams of headlights moving down the walls were night too.

Above the couch, the long upswept arc of a lit cigarette. The red tip moved. It took deep, burning breaths. I saw blackness on blackness. I backed away, down the long corridor of that night, my feet kicking bottles of whiskey and rattling scattered cans, until years later, I found that the front door had been left open and that I could reverse my whole body through it.

A therapist told me that some people walk into the same buildings again and again.

Isn't there a way to learn differently? I wanted to know.

She smiled and said attractions can't be changed.

Well, maybe that's true, because I did careen into another night in my midthirties. He was a professor of Southern history. Small and ill-tempered. After a football game, he threw a bottle at where I'd stood a moment earlier. He took after me in his big, beat-up truck, honking while I bolted through yards and gardens. When I reached the river, I slowed and followed it home.

I heard what my therapist said, but I can counter with this: the red trace of the cigarette, the thrown bottle—I stayed only long enough but to see. By the time things turned to ash and the glass shattered, I was gone, and I try to focus on that.

10.

Which reminds me: When I was eleven years old, I watched as my mother performed a rapid reversal. She hurried out of a long and narrow blackness until she reached daylight, at which point she turned, grabbed my hand, and started running fast and forward.

After my parents separated, my mother was done with marriage. She did not say it, but demonstrated. She has been dating the same man for close to twenty-five years. They live apart—oceans apart—but visit each other throughout the year.

Katharine Hepburn: *Sometimes I wonder if men and women really suit each other. Perhaps they should live next door and just visit now and then.*

But, as a teenager, I unhappily, foolishly perceived my mother's relationship with her boyfriend as a luckless and odd one.

My father, on the other hand, married another seven times. I was not so foolish as to misconstrue that as luck.

11.

Here is one from the Lusitania that squeezes my heart:

Still on deck with a few people. The last boats have left. We are sinking fast. Some men near me are praying with a priest. The end is near. Maybe this note will . . .

So many possibilities.

The ship sank in eighteen minutes. The author was never located, was presumed drowned off the coast of Ireland. Only four and a half lines rising, like a last breath.

Yearning after infinite possibilities, I am only capable of inventing one: *Maybe this note will reach you.*

12.

It is an oversimplification to say that a few midnights gone all tooth and claw prompted my retreat to a cool and quiet twilight.

The habitable world can be an aggression. A misophonic minefield. Recall reading as a child your favorite book and having someone interrupt, how your interior world collapsed. There is a man. He screams absurdly. His office is near mine. Every day, he walks in and screams, *Hey neighbor!* I cannot help but think the scream is pure in its motives, designed to create panic.

Having taken myself off the summer teaching schedule for the first time, I sit on the porch swing and reread Janet Frame. A fan spins slowly from the blue ceiling above me. Painted that sweet blue to scare away the haints, my father's old nanny used to tell me of her porch ceiling. Mosquitos blacken my legs, and the ice in my glass vanishes in seconds. My hope is that isolation — the act of going away from the world — is not always risky. That it doesn't always cost something of the mind. Because the fear is as Frame describes: *. . . hours and years spent in the factories, the streets, the cathedrals of the imagination, learning the unique functioning of Mirror City, its skies and space, its own planetary system, without stopping to think that one may become homeless in the world, and bankrupt, abandoned by the Envoy.*

13.

Yesterday was the repose of sun heating water, surf fetching in long, sweeping lines to shore, the great, honking awks of startled herons in the sound, and the wind running faster as the morning, flitted with the shadows of speeding clouds, grew and passed. Inside my body was an endless spray of light. Outside of my body, salt gathered in familiar scales on my skin.

Nevertheless, as we all sometimes do, I feel tired. Fatigued. And I have this lump in my throat.

Is your depression spiking? asks the psychiatrist. She is slight and pretty and soft-spoken. Her husband was a classmate of mine, and we spend part of every session chatting about their children.

It's hard to tell? I add that learning what is an appropriate degree of sadness or fear is difficult.

My aphasic tendencies are worsening too and, while that is more disquieting, I hesitate over telling her. I type vanishment instead of banishment. I like becomes a light. I am traveling light becomes I am a traveling light.

I tell her my tongue is swollen.

She wants to see it.

I stick out my tongue. It retains the imprint of my teeth.

You have angioedema, she says. Consulting a screen to her left, she remarks, *It's a side-effect.*

Because I am more concerned about the bouts of fatigue, the cognitive slowness, and a general ambivalence toward the society of people—men in particular—I forget to ask, a side-effect of what?

I am newly uninterested in romantic company. In marriage. *Even in sex,* I tell her. But I don't mind it really. It's all the other people who care. And I just want to make sure it's okay that I don't care. That it's not a symptom of something.

She needs to know if I felt differently before my sickness.

I say, *Yes, differently.*

She needs to know if I experience moments of joy.

I cannot bring myself to tell her that when joy happens, it splits me like lightning. I cannot say his name.

I ask, instead, if it is possible to be between. I say the thing about being between my selves. I show her my notes about light: In developing his quantum theory, Einstein suggests, mathematically, that electrons attached to atoms in a metal can absorb a specific quantity of light (first termed a quantum but later renamed a photon) and, he concludes, *thus have the energy to escape.*

It doesn't matter how many times I study the lines, all I can apprehend is that light provides us with the energy to get away.

I say to the doctor, *The next time someone asks what I am doing with my life, my answer will be: I am a photon absorbing light for my next escape.*

There is a pause as I reach for something. *I am,* I announce triumphantly, aphasia on overdrive, *a traveling light.*

Before leaving, I mention the lump in my throat. The one that comes and goes but has now been staying, waking me up from the inside at night, reminding me not to sleep flat but to prop myself up on pillows while the dog gathers himself into my side so that together we wait in this posture for morning.

14.

I had forgotten why engagement rings are worn on the third finger, but it came back to me as I watered the hydrangeas this morning. The *vena amori*, or vein of love, was believed to run from this finger straight to the heart. We know now that the ring doesn't touch a vein; it touches a nerve.

My mother never had engagement or wedding jewelry. I thought she did because there was a ring on her finger, thin and gold and looped into a lover's knot. The metal was soft; twisting and snarling easily. At some point, I learned she had ordered it for herself out of a catalog. By and by, she lost the ring. When I offered to find another, a replacement, she shook her head no.

Is this significant: Sometimes I see him swimming in the winter ocean. Other times, I notice his car, abandoned in an empty beach lot, black tie-downs whipping away from the roof racks.

I want to say that I did not set out here to write about love, not in the least — not about love, the institutions we've constructed to house it, or the ways in which we attempt to escape it.

But here I am, caught in the act of coming back.

Spook science. That is what we talked about under the string lights. A decade had elapsed when I pulled off I-40 in a rainstorm, parked under an overpass, and listened to a whole program on quantum entanglement. At around midnight, I sent him a letter: *Ten years after I sat with you on a dock at Holden, under the little lights talking about the big bang, about particles and how they might recognize each other, I would hear on the radio, a special about quantum entanglement. Every particle has a twin, and even if the two are separated, even if they're far away, they respond to one another.*

He wrote, *There was a wind today it reminded me of you. There was a sunrise, the beach, the distance, the clarity of the horizon—*

He wrote, *Where does an atom keep its heart? It is all mystifying — much like the timing of this communication from you because I did something this past Sunday before I knew of the existence of this email — I read through the pieces of my past — our past. I was reading when you sent me this.*

I was reading through poems and stories I had written nearly ten years ago and do you know what I discovered? You were at the end of every sentence.

15.

The socks I stole from the hospital come up to my knees. They are dotted with little, white rubber-traction pads on all sides, which kept me from sliding off the X-ray table. The room was satisfyingly cold. The doctor and nurse were so nice I wished we could know each other outside of a radiology clinic. The one thing to which they would not agree was letting me take the bright blue scrubs home with me.

People are always *asking that,* the nurse said.

The X-ray table tilted and spun in wondrous ways with me clinging to it. In the end, the experience would have been pleasant and like something out of *The Little Prince* if it weren't for the barium they kept making me swallow. The test was to image my throat, to locate the obstruction my doctor had felt there. Other orders include endoscopies and biopsies.

Ask for a twilight endoscopy, writes a friend from Georgia. It's when they knock you out but not all the way.

I am charmed by the name but reluctant to follow through on the additional exams. The ultrasound of my thyroid turned up nothing, and tests are expensive. Distracting the doctors, too, is my tongue, which remains mysteriously larger than it should be. I bite lightly on it when my mouth is closed. When I say *ahhh*, you can count every tooth by the scalloped dent it leaves. I am beginning to suspect myself of being hypochondriacal, stuffed with a fiction that is outgrowing my body.

16.

Today felt like early spring, cool and with the sun chancing upon the under-arcs of the dogwood leaves. With my dog, Seamus, trotting up ahead on his long leash, I chased the light and, just when I felt the world was all shadow, we turned a corner and blinked into a lower sun.

We walked in lieu of attending a party.

We went close to the festivities, which were nearby, only a few streets over. We went all the way up to the iron side-gate and, through the hedges, everyone looked delighted, and children tore about, shrieking, with tangled hair and juice boxes, and my friend's husband played a toy ukulele, and the sound followed us, tinny and young, as we rambled away and down the wide, quiet streets of my father's boyhood neighborhood.

I stopped by my grandmother's small memorial garden in Forest Hills. More stone step than flower, but the tribute has the permanence of home. My father, who left decades ago and without a glance back, raised me on a boat called *Slow Dancer*. Our crossing was through a thousand landscapes. I am returned here, to this port city, because its rhythm and pulse are familiar as my own voice and blood. I know the water here. The way it heats and cools and where in the channel it switches flow. Only with this unshifting geography can I middle, can I banish myself to the suspended maze of my interior. And the idea is indeed lovely in its sound.

So many years gone by in a flash. The couple who sent out the messages in bottles divorced, and I no longer know them. I was sick, and then got better. One day, tomorrow or decades from tomorrow, I will be sick again. I have dated men, some of whom I even lived with for a time. I can't argue that all there is to show for my residence in this world are some words stuttering slowly on the page, a rented house, a pair of rescued pets, a low-paying job at an out-of-the-way university, and a few hours salted away to which I return on nights like this.

I have whiled away hours in old books and photographs in a mulish and mawkish nostalgia. The stereo spills a frail jazz. The cicadas are humming a low-voltage sound. Small wonder that every now and then a horse of sadness circles in me, restless, nickering fearfully in the dim.

17.

I looked up the longest recorded engagement. Octavio Guillan and Adriana Martinez. The couple lingered in a sixty-seven-year engagement before marrying at age eighty-two.

Maybe it isn't normal, my not craving and lusting and desiring.

It is not normal, my doctor confirms. But that's okay. It's okay to rest, she says.

This is an accounting of dusk as I am knowing it. It has been years since I have been with him in the bluing light. I have never cried over not having him, not once, because I love him outside of having. I won't be between forever, but who can predict how much less.

I hold onto this: Out on the ocean with my parents, before my mother sped into a reversal, when the sky was clear and fell around us in a perfect circle, we gathered on deck to watch for a flash. The world held its breath, and we did too, and surely all the osprey in the world hung with their wings flapping ever so slowly as the sun went down. At the last moment, my mother would put her hand on my shoulder, and my father would say, *Hannah, look,* and the distance—the future—breathed a bright green light, and we went into night, certain it would be lit with stars.

18.

. . . I feel like I am disobeying God in the time between.

Well, I think that is the most persuasive love letter ever written. The oldest message ever sent. And what a hope, that everything not wild and perfect is between. In this lapse of obedience, I am catching my breath so that I can lose it later.

I am now a photon, next a traveling light, and there is a shape loping through the trees hard to make out.

HANNAH DELA CRUZ ABRAMS was awarded the 2013 Whiting Writers Award for her novella *The Man Who Danced with Dolls* and her memoir-in-progress *The Following Sea.* She has received a Rona Jaffe National Literary Award and a North Carolina Arts Council Fellowship. Her work has most recently appeared in *Carolina Quarterly, Oxford American,* and the *Southern Humanities Review.* She teaches in the English department at the University of North Carolina at Wilmington.

On Second Thought

DANA SACHS

IN THE SUMMER OF 1996, my husband, Todd, and I rented a Ryder van in San Francisco, filled it with our belongings, and drove across the country so that he could take a position as a professor at the University of North Carolina at Wilmington. It was a dream come true for him. For me, not so much. My writing centered on Asia, and San Francisco was reasonably close to that region, plus I adored the crazy cultural mix of the place. Practically speaking, though, I didn't have to be there. While I could write from just about anywhere, Todd needed a place to profess. We agreed to try Wilmington for a year. If I hated it, we'd move back to San Francisco and Todd would go to law school.

For the first 2700 miles of our cross-country drive, I focused on the adventure. I'm a traveller at heart, so any new place gives me a thrill. Cranking up Bob Dylan (his) or Neil Young (mine) on the little tape recorder that sat between our seats, we passed through the Nevada desert, the Rocky Mountains, the soft green carpet of the prairie, the Mississippi Delta, the hills of East Tennessee. Then, on that last stretch of plain between Charlotte and Wilmington — stop-and-start traffic and strip malls followed by empty fields and spindly stands of pine — I began to cry. Oh, for San Francisco's bougainvillea and its hills. We stopped and bought boiled peanuts by the side of the road. When we pulled up in front of the house we'd rented in Wilmington, I threw up.

Those were a difficult first few months, though I could acknowledge, even then, that Wilmington had charm. The beaches were close to perfect and the downtown had Spanish moss, effervescent porches, and a river with a creepy name. I'm a Southerner myself, so I slid right into the languid pace, appreciated how, even in a crowded grocery store, people didn't race through with their carts, grabbing things. No, in Wilmington people strolled. And I loved that when you walked by someone on the street, acquaintance or stranger, you looked each other in the eye and said hello.

But the city wasn't cosmopolitan. Diversity seemed almost entirely measured by black or white, and those two colors rarely mixed. Whenever I found myself in the belly of the city — that shopping center underworld of Kmart and Bojangles and car dealerships — I felt that the Monster of Suburbia had swallowed me whole. Hadn't I originally moved to San Francisco to get away from all of that?

That first summer, we spent an evening at the home of Betsy, one of Todd's new university colleagues, eating limp and tasteless take-out Chinese. Betsy came from Nebraska, lived in a ranch house with a two-car garage, seemed content with the life that she and her husband, a fellow professor, had made here. While Todd and Betsy talked about online grading systems and teacher-student ratios, I picked at a rubbery snow pea, longed for my favorite San Francisco noodle shop, thought maybe I should die right there. Somehow, I had become one of those trapped spouses whose partner finds the perfect job in a place where the other member of the couple doesn't want to be.

But here I am, nearly twenty years later, still living in Wilmington. The question I ask myself is not "Why didn't we leave?" but "Why have I been happy here?" Because I have been happy, though it took me a long time—years, really—to realize that.

In autumn along the Carolina coast, the maples explode in crimson color. Winter arrives and I can see my breath. Spring offers a parade of flowering trees—redwood, tulip, dogwood, plum, and cherry. Summer turns the air into a sultry mix of gardenia, jasmine, sunscreen, and lemony tea. Wilmington has an extra season, too—Hurricane, which, on occasion, unfurls its own dramatic narrative of storm-naming, duct-taping, and battery-hoarding, followed by hours huddled around the radio, peeking out at the gray-green sky, the wind and rain, the elements raging. And then, finally, calm returns and we venture outside to step across the downed tree trunks and the power lines lying like snakes along the sidewalks, and to contemplate the extent of the cleanup, the hours or days we may go without power. At dusk, we contribute our steak and chicken to a spontaneous neighborhood potluck, organized so that we might all consume the contents of refrigerators and freezers before everything spoils in the heat. In California, we barely knew our neighbors' names.

We had a son, bought a house, had another son, bought a different house, this one with a yard where they could roam. First impressions, I learned, can be deceiving. Betsy and her husband had a daughter, and our friendship deepened during the afternoons we followed our toddlers into the woods behind her house, became pirates, stooped over snails, poked sticks into the muddy muck while talking, simultaneously, about racism, income inequality, and global warming. Yes, she came from Nebraska, but she had also lived in France, met a rock star at a concert, and, for a time, ran away with him. All in all, not so boring, not so suburban. She had one of the sharpest minds of anyone I ever met, a scathing wit, and fierce commitment to making the world better. She also had a set of tiny little silver spoons with which, one winter evening, we ate homemade chocolate mousse. I loved her for all of that.

Big cities have thousands of spirited and fascinating people. We don't have as many of those people here, but—I learned this from my friend

Doc, a network television producer who moved down from New York—you don't actually have room in your life for thousands of spirited and fascinating people. You only have room for ten or twenty of them, and we have plenty more than that. We have writers and yogis, environmental activists, orthodox Jews, surfers, entrepreneurs, Shakespearean actors, fashion designers, sommeliers, brain scientists, filmmakers, classical pianists, Sudanese, Brazilians, Africans, Jamaicans, food stylists, pharmaceutical researchers, championship swimmers, master carpenters, community activists, and television stars here and there, too.

We have enough, I discovered, to stimulate and surprise.

Home is not so much a geographical point on a map as it is a set of places that inspire memories in us. Here is the downtown carriage tour, which my older son, Jesse, as a toddler, used to call the Big White Horse. Here is Empie Park, where we spent innumerable hours on the swings, ate innumerable Goldfish, tossed innumerable grapes. And Greenfield Lake, where I used to jog with my friend Beau, and where he once accidentally came around a scrim of azalea and interrupted a couple in the midst of indiscretion.

And here is my local grocery, where one day I ran into and chatted with so many fellow parents from my kids' school that I left feeling like I'd attended a PTA meeting. And here is Los Portales Supermercado, where we like to pick up fresh tamales on weekends; and Genki Sushi, where the Japanese proprietors pass out homemade caramels for dessert; and Saigon Market, where my husband once told the owner, "If your store did not exist in this town, our family would have to move." Over the years since we arrived, Wilmington's growing population has increased its diversity, adding depth and breadth, deepening the colors of its rainbow. A vibrant interfaith refugee resettlement network has welcomed so many new immigrants that we now have a significant community of Burmese. And in many, many restaurants and bakeries, neighborhoods and workplaces, Spanish is the spoken language. I love that.

Not all my memories are happy ones. Here is the tennis court where my son Sam broke his arm. Here is the bridge from which we tossed flowers after I miscarried. Here is the parking lot where a college student was murdered for $5 and a submarine sandwich, and the corner where a young child got caught in the crossfire. Here is the print shop where I ordered photocopies one afternoon in 2001, and, after filling in the date on the form — September 11 — the clerk said, "Well, I guess we'll always remember that one."

This is just my life, the way I journey through this city after all these years. These are my "joys and concerns," as they call it at my children's Quaker school. Here is the chair I was sitting in when I heard about the lump in Betsy's breast. Here is the Sunoco station where I filled the car with gas, fingers numb with cold, the day that she felt strong enough to drive to Raleigh to see a Monet exhibit. Here is the oncology center, with its bubbling fountain and seaside palette, where she spent too many afternoons. Here is where they held her memorial service, her husband and little daughter sitting up in front. Here is the house where she doesn't live anymore.

My older son leaves for college this year. Before too long, the younger one will go as well. They are children of this city and, to prove it, we still have one of those teeny tiny onesies emblazoned with the words Cape Fear Hospital that Jesse was wearing when we brought him home. My boys don't speak with Southern accents, but they have a manner, a slowness and friendliness, a way of shaking hands and looking people in the eye, that connects them, somehow, to this place where they grew up. Wherever they go, I think they'll take that with them.

People say that you put down roots. I don't think I've put down roots here, and I don't discount the possibility that I will leave some day. Rather, I have allowed the city to grow up around me, spread its tendrils and branches through my life. Wilmington and I have passed through seasons together. In this city, I have watched the fall of blazing leaves and the new shoots blossom.

DANA SACHS, a native of Memphis, is the author of the novels *If You Lived Here* and *The Secret of the Nightingale Palace,* and two books of nonfiction, *The Life We Were Given: Operation Babylift, International Adoption and the Children of War in Vietnam* and *The House on Dream Street: Memoir of an American Woman in Vietnam.* Her articles and essays have appeared in many publications, including *National Geographic, Travel and Leisure Family,* and the *International Herald Tribune.* In 2006, she served as a Fulbright Scholar in Hanoi. She teaches at UNC Wilmington.

The Miracle of the Superama Magic Dreydl

KAREN E. BENDER

Dear Mr. CEO of Superama America,
the Company That Created the Superama Magic Dreydl:

I WOULD LIKE TO LODGE A COMPLAINT against the Superama Magic
Dreydl, which I purchased at Party City last week. We were making our
annual pilgrimage to the store, gazing upon the holiday decorations. We
saw the Superama animated Santa's elf that could toss candy at you,
Christmas trees constructed of shiny green, white, red, pink, and silver that
sang "The Little Drummer Boy" and "Silent Night," a lawn reindeer made
of white lights that raised its head and stared at you with bright red eyes,
candy canes that sang "Jingle Bells."

This was a bit of a charged little trip, Mr. CEO — Party City reserves
one-quarter of one shelf for Hanukkah decorations; and there are three
full aisles for the marvelous Christmas ones. This is a little hard for Rachel
because, Owner of Superama Products, Rachel is the only Jewish child in
our school in Wilmington, North Carolina, and one of a handful in New
Hanover County, and it was December again.

So I was looking at the various products on the Hanukkah shelf. The Maccabeans (jelly beans colored silver), the menorah water globe, which, when you shake it, weirdly snows, the yo-yo singing an electronic version of "O Hanukkah" that sounds a little like the buzzing of a gnat.

I'm a low-tech person myself. I actually like the quiet, somewhat pyromaniacal aspect of the candles on the menorah, seeing them in the window. But my daughter was having none of it. She'd had a long day at school, trying not to say anything when her classmates talked about how Santa liked the cookies they left out for him. She told me on the way home that it's obviously the parents giving the cookies, and are they the ones making him fat? And if he's fat, how does he get down the chimney? I didn't know the answer. Christmas had its own wonderful stories and characters, mesmerizing in their own way, but here they tend to be the only ones we hear. So I wanted something to make our holiday seem nice, too, not competitive really, because we know the values of Hanukkah and Christmas are about other, more noble issues, of course. But when you're eight years old, and you're looking at a package of Maccabeans and a lighted, nodding reindeer, who wins? I ask you. Who?

Plus there had been an incident with Edwin, the wild boy in the class who was, more often than not, told to go sit in "the office"—the polite name for the timeout zone. He asked Rachel why she didn't believe in Santa, and she said, because he's not real, and Edwin said, yes he is and he comes on his reindeer and brings me everything in the *world!* He shouted the word *world*, which got him sent back to the office. And Rachel got upset, though I knew he actually didn't get everything he wanted. What have the holidays become for parents but a season of keeping back a wave of torrential greed?

So off we went to Party City—to find something that would cheer her up.

Rachel knelt down at the Hanukkah shelf and rummaged through various items. Then she found the Superama Magic Dreydl. On the package it said, "Buy this dreydl. Now! Spin it! Fly it! Create a miracle! Win the dreydl game!"

It looked like an ordinary dreydl with its pointed end, the letters *Nun, Gimel, Hay,* and *Shin* carved on the sides. The dreydl made a low, buzzing sound, as though trying to figure out what song to play, and flashed a brilliant white light when you squeezed it.

"I want this!" she said.

Mr. CEO — I am the parental Hanukkah ambassador for Rachel's class each year, a role I take quite seriously. I tell them the story of the Maccabees who fought to take back the Temple when the Romans took it over, and how the menorah candles burned for eight nights when there was just enough oil for one night. I bring in the menorah and the dreydls for the students to play with. So that day at Party City, I bought five Superama Magic Dreydls. We walked to the parking lot, Rachel clutching her new Hanukkah-shelf acquisition, which was still emitting a sound, though not anything we recognized as a holiday song.

I wanted that dreydl to be magic. I wanted it to do something grand for Rachel. I wanted something to happen when she squeezed that dreydl and the light exploded in it, something so that she felt a little less left out.

When we got home, we tried out that dreydl. There were no instructions for the magic dreydl, something I would strongly advise you include in the future. We waited for it to do something miraculous. Such as fly. Mr. CEO, this dreydl did not fly. It barely spun. It played no song I could identify. It bounced. "It does *nothing!*" Rachel shrieked and threw it across the room, despondent. It would impress no one.

I told her that we had to go over the basics for my presentation to the class — how to light the menorah, what the letters *Nun, Gimel, Hay,* and *Shin* mean, the story of the Maccabees, how it is good to stand up for what you believe. Rachel was having none of it. "The magic dreydl is the least magic thing there is," she cried. Things were devolving, Mr. CEO.

Nevertheless, we marched into Rachel's classroom for the presentation the next week, menorah and dreydls in hand. Her classmates sat on the floor, waiting. They were excited. They had heard about the possibility of chocolate gelt, a rumor I had fostered. They were eager listeners. They watched as I put the candles in the menorah (unfortunately, I couldn't light them due to school fire laws). They had questions. Did Hanukkah offer the same gift opportunities as Christmas and how did the candles burn on and on and was she old enough to light them herself and how many presents did Rachel get, etc.? They listened to the story. Then they were put into small groups to play dreydl.

So, dreydl. I was never quite sure how to play the dreydl game, to be perfectly honest. I never listened that closely in religious school. I knew that you had a pot of goodies in the middle of the circle and if the dreydl landed on *Nun,* you got none of it, *Hay,* you got half the pot, *Gimel,* you got it all, and *Shin* you added a goody to the pot. The pot disappeared quickly and I had to keep replenishing it. Then there was the fact that I didn't know what items to put in the pot—the chocolate gelt would cause a riot, pennies would mysteriously vanish. So I settled, rather boringly, on dried beans. They were playing with piles of kidney beans, which was not that satisfying, and the teachers were eyeing the beans skittering away from the pot under desks. Rachel sat with her group as each one spun a Superama Magic Dreydl, which did not seem any more remarkable, and she watched as some of the other kids stopped spinning the dreydls to grab handfuls of beans and start throwing them with glee.

And then Edwin spoke.

"I want a dreydl!" he said.

He had just returned from the office before the dreydl game started and had not had a chance to play.

"Wait, Edwin," said the teacher.

"But I want one!" he said. "I've never seen one before."

A small group sitting by him looked like they were wracked with confusion; he leaned forward and grabbed a dreydl. He stared at it and squeezed it; the light flashed through the room.

"Edwin!" called the teacher. "You have not behaved well enough to earn privileges today! You cannot play with that dreydl! Put it down this instant!"

But Edwin was not giving up that dreydl. He ran to the corner of the room and squeezed it again, watching its lights flash. He lowered it to the ground and spun it.

The dreydl twirled.

Edwin had some sort of amazing flick in his wrist, so the dreydl twirled. And twirled. Edwin was, shockingly, the best dreydl spinner of anyone. Rachel was amazed. The other students stopped and watched and wondered what it would land on. Would Edwin get nothing? Half? Everything? What? It was a quiet, simmering moment, almost a magical one, and then the dreydl landed.

Gimel.

"What does that mean?" Edwin asked, softly.

"You get everything," said Rachel.

"You mean all these beans?" asked Edwin. "I don't want those. I want the dreydl. I want Santa to bring me a dreydl."

Rachel looked all at once happy. "Santa can't bring you a dreydl," said Rachel.

Edwin looked crestfallen. "Then who can?"

"Me," said Rachel.

Edwin looked at her with an expression of something she had not seen in awhile: amazement.

"Can I keep the dreydl?" he asked.

"If you say thank you," she said. "Nicely."

Edwin clasped the dreydl to his chest and said thank you, nicely, and Rachel beamed. The dreydl letters: *Nes Gadol Haya Sham*—A great miracle happened there. But maybe it could happen here, too. Maybe Edwin would want a dreydl.

So Mr. CEO, I am just writing you to complain about this one aspect of the Superama Magic Dreydl: When we took the rest of them home and tried to spin them, NONE of them spun the way Edwin's did. I don't know what happened. And we never figured out how to make them fly.

But thankfully, it didn't matter. Rachel hasn't complained any more this year about Hanukkah. She even asked to light the menorah by herself.

So I have just one thing to say to you, Mr. CEO: Next year, step up production.

KAREN E. BENDER is the author of the story collection *Refund* and the novels *Like Normal People* and *Town of Empty Rooms.* Her fiction has appeared in *The New Yorker, Granta, Plough-shares, Zoetrope,* and *Guernica,* and has been reprinted in *Best American Short Stories, Best American Mystery Stories, New Stories from the South: The Year's Best,* and won two Pushcart Prizes. Her story "Refund" was shortlisted for the Frank O'Connor International Short Story Prize.

A World Apart

Animals

JOHN JEREMIAH SULLIVAN

1.

HALF A MILE FROM OUR HOUSE there's a little gas market, run by
friendly Russians—Siberians, a few of them—whose presence in southeastern North Carolina remains inexplicable to me, and seemingly to them
many days. Men in three neighborhoods make needless stops for glimpses
of the register girls. The place stocks maybe sixty flavors of blunt and
a lot of dusty off-brand merchandise. One often has encounters there or
witnesses little scenes. On that morning, as I stood in front of the coolers on the far wall, choosing a ginger-ale brand, a girl walked in. Had there
been a vinyl record playing, it would have scratched to a stop. Wearing jean
shorts and a white tank-top undershirt, bone structure pure Scandinavian
huntress, pale lank hair hanging. While the few of us already in there stared,
a different creature sort of materialized in the sunlit door behind her.
A shirtless man, in his prematurely aged fifties, with a beach-burnt
face caved in on itself from toothlessness and wrong choices. Wearing
a Gilligan-style hat and track-suit bottoms, flapping penguin-like in
sandals, almost a Gabby Hayes aspect. Was he following her? No . . . they

were together. As she got closer, I saw bruises on her limbs, and something off about her eyes. She seemed to stare at nothing. Messed up. They came and stood beside me. "God dammit!" the man hollered, as if addressing the entire store. "What's the matter, Daddy?" she said. Her slurred drawl verged on a purr. This person was not her father. I was looking through a brief window into some vastly dark trailer-park-pimp scenario. "They ain't got no goddamn Fanta is what's wrong!" he cried. They left quickly.

2.

Walking home from the market in the summer, I had a meeting with a man who looked every bit of eighty. Dark black skin with a steel-gray beard, no shirt, wearing a shapeless cap of some kind. He stood beside a bicycle and was cursing at it, picking it up just a half inch from the road and slamming it down. The chain was hanging, touching the pavement. The bike had fishing gear all over it in plastic bags. I drew up even with him and asked if I could help. "Yeah," he said, "do something about that god-damn devil." Not pointing at or indicating anything in particular, only this world, which even the Bible allows is Satan's to run. As I walked away he called out, "I wish the devil was a man, so I could chop him up and use him for shrimp bait!"

3.

There's a tidal creek two hundred yards from our house called Burnt Mill Creek. It used to be called Mill Creek, we were told, but the mill burnt (a century ago), so it's Burnt Mill Creek. We walk along it two or three times a week. Cypress groves grow beside its banks. The trees put up strange knobby above-ground roots, called knees, the purpose of which scientists don't understand. All sorts of toxic effluent runs into this water, biologists at the local college say, but the stream is full of life anyway. Fish, frogs, herons, dragonflies, fiddler crabs.

Also human beings. In the early mornings, people sit on overturned white buckets in the mist and fish with spinning rods for crap fish,

"German carp," species like that, meat you have to salt and fry forever before you can eat it.

There's a snapping turtle the size of a manhole, legendary in the neighborhood, but real—I saw it once, with my daughter Maria, when she was smaller. It lay on the muddy bank, already slithering backward toward the water when we came upon it. She saw its enormous prehistoric beak and thought it looked like an owl and called it Owl Turtle. Owl Turtle starred in her crayon drawings for a year.

Mainly the life in the creek is benign, to us at least, but lately we have experienced a disturbing rise in sightings of dangerous creatures. Last week a medium-sized black bear appeared. Keep in mind this is the middle of town. The animal frightened off a bunch of fishermen. One man had been too scared to return for his pole, and it lay there until the next day, when it disappeared. Later that same afternoon I met one of my neighbors from a block over, walking his dog through the cypresses. He looked shaken. He said that he and the dog had just narrowly avoided stepping on a water moccasin (highly venomous) moving through the grass.

Most noticeably, this very afternoon, a six-foot alligator showed up, floating right there in the shade of one of the concrete bridges that span the creek. A group of people had gathered to stare at it. Gators rarely come up so far from the marshes.

"Got a camera?" one woman asked. I had my phone. I took a pic, and then everyone gave me their email addresses, and I sent them the pic while we stood there, the gator appearing to watch us with its cold and yellow-green saurian eyes. "There you go," I said to the folks. "I sent it." And walked home wondering if we should move.

4.

Last night we were visiting friends but stayed in a hotel (didn't want our youngest, still a baby, waking them in the night). Their six-year-old son, who gets along with our older daughter, stayed with us. The two kids camped in the coffee-table room. But an hour after lights out, we could still hear them talking, keeping each other awake with nonsensical jokes. About 11:30 my wife sends me in: "You have to get them to sleep. This is insane." I'm lying horizontally across the foot of their bed. They have their heads on their respective pillows. I don't have any real books, but I have my phone, so I get on Google Books, and bring up my favorite story from the six-year-old period, *The Swiss Family Robinson* (top bunk, flashlight, heaven). I start reading in the dark. The shipwreck. The frightened praying on deck. The cowardly crew that rows off, taking the lifeboats. I remember it all. The boy falls asleep instantly, in a mummy posture, and for a few minutes I think mine's out, too—I keep reading just to make sure she's down-down—but then she starts asking questions, mostly about unfamiliar words, and I realize she's listening. They're sawing the casks in half to make their tub-boat, preparing to flee the doomed ship.

Suddenly she sits bolt upright. He face is a ghostly blue-white in the glow of the phone. It's as if she's briefly fallen asleep and had a bad dream. She holds up two fingers.

"I have two questions," she says.

"*Mm-hmm?*"

"First question: Who's speaking?"

"What do you mean?"

"In the story, who is it who's telling the story?"

"Oh, it's the father. He never says who he is, you're just supposed to assume . . ."

She nods, absorbing that.

"Second question."

"Go ahead."

"Is this a family of robins?"

5.

Working at the dining room table I hear my daughter going off down the hallway, and she's singing to herself a song that she knows from her Quaker grade school, a song about an early Quaker named George Fox.

Part of it goes, "'In my old leather breeches and my shaggy shaggy locks, I am walking in the glory of the Light,' said Fox."

Remembering her question about the robins, I took a chance, and said, "Maria, when you sing that song, do you imagine an actual fox, with shaggy locks?"

"Well," she said in her precise way, "I have always wondered."

Born in Louisville, Kentucky, **JOHN JEREMIAH SULLIVAN** has lived in Wilmington for the past eleven years. He was an editor at the *Oxford American* and *Harper's Magazine* and a writer for *GQ* before becoming a contributing writer for the *New York Times Magazine*. His essay collection *Pulphead* was a bestseller and made numerous year-end Top 10 lists. He is currently the Southern editor of the *Paris Review*. His next book, *The Prime Minister of Paradise*, will be published in 2016.

Spin

SHEILA WEBSTER BONEHAM

Here on this spit of sand I kneel,
south wind to my back, and watch. The wild Atlantic roars
to my right and tosses remains of jellyfish and clam, oyster, fish
guts, sea glass, flat-eyed tern, flotsam and wrack. And to my left
a runaway thread of salt and water murmurs its way
through mudflat, grass, and sedge.

I might turn east to the blue-green reach
where anything can be when the language of light
throws poems over the roll and heave, and dolphins leap,
and cormorants dive, and surfacing sparks
skip over mortal shadows,

or west, to the beckoning marsh
where sun-drenched rivers glide into oncoming dusk, twist
gypsy skirts against the dark—scarlet, tangerine, bronze, mauve.
They dance and spin for a moment, and slip like quiet
into rising night. Mourning dove coos, *Safe harbor here, here,*
here in the coming night.

Barred owl *whoos* a somewhere prayer,
eyes the dove, and there in the grass a heron twists
her thread of a neck. She waits, foot cocked, wing tensed, eye
sharp as light,
and strikes.

Pie-billed grebe glides seaward,
breast to the incoming tide, aware, unperturbed.
She spins a notch, dark muscle on glittering chop. She starts
at the sound of tussle in the grass. And there,
where breakers occlude the calm,
she spins again.

SHEILA WEBSTER BONEHAM writes across genres, often about animals, environment, gender, and culture in the anthropological sense. She has published seventeen nonfiction books and four novels. Her essays and poems have appeared in *2015 Best Science and Nature Writing*, *Red Earth Review*, *The Wayfarer*, and elsewhere. Her work has won multiple Maxwell and MUSE awards for fiction and nonfiction, the Prime Number Magazine Award for Creative Nonfiction, and has been nominated for the Pushcart Prize.

Love & Death in the Cape Fear Serpentarium

WENDY BRENNER

> *He is a fool who injures himself by amassing things.*
> *And no one knows why people cannot help but do it.*
> —Translation of anonymous *Le danse macabre* verse, Paris, 1485

> *Fortunately, I number among my friends a young man named Dean Ripa, who could*
> *have stepped from the pages of a Joseph Conrad novel.*
> —William S. Burroughs, *The Western Lands*

ONE DAY IN 1971 in Wilmington, North Carolina, fourteen-year-old Dean Ripa was at home performing surgery on a cottonmouth snake, and it bit him. This was unfortunate for a couple of reasons. He knew enough about snakes to know he would probably not die, but he did need a ride to the hospital, which meant his parents were going to find out about the fifty snakes he was keeping in their spare room: rattlesnakes, water moccasins he'd caught in local swamps, even several cobras he had purchased via mail order—he had a king cobra years before he had his driver's license.

The bite landed him in intensive care for two weeks—with fever, a grossly swollen arm, blistering skin—during which time his father donated his entire snake collection to a local roadside zoo, a seemingly apocalyptic setback that might have ended any normal person's love affair with snakes. But Dean turned out to be another kind of person, the kind who, after a full recovery, quickly began amassing more snakes, breeding his own snakes and making extra money to buy snakes by collecting snakes for the same zoo that had adopted his earlier snakes. A year after the cottonmouth episode, one of his new cobras got loose and the whole Ripa family had to move out of the house for five days until it could be found and shot.

Thirty years later, in what might be the ultimate fantasy of young snake-lovers everywhere, Dean Ripa opened the Cape Fear Serpentarium, and, most thrilling of all, to a twelve-year-old acquaintance of mine, he lives there, too.

The Serpentarium is no roadside attraction, but an elegant, bi-level, 6300-square-foot gallery overlooking the Cape Fear River in gentrified downtown Wilmington, exhibiting the largest collection of live exotic venomous snakes in the U.S.—about a hundred on public display at any given time, representing dozens of different species—almost all of which were captured by Dean himself in jungles and marshes around the world. He specializes in the rarest and deadliest: Gaboon vipers, black mambas, spitting cobras, puff adders, and bushmasters, of which he has the biggest known collection anywhere. In fact, Dean was the first person ever to breed the rare black-headed bushmaster in captivity (he continues to supply them internationally to zoos and researchers), and once even reproduced a bushmaster hybrid, in effect recreating an extinct ancestor of the existing species. He has also survived four bushmaster bites—"envenomings" is the herpetologist's Orwellian term—despite the fact that almost all bushmaster victims die, even with antivenom treatment.

Amazingly enough, the Serpentarium was built by Dean's father, a local contractor, who has presumably forgiven Dean for his adolescence (or perhaps is just happy to have survived it). The Serpentarium's neighbors include antique stores and historic-plaqued bed-and-breakfasts and Thai restaurants and art galleries, and I wonder about the neighborhood reaction to the snake museum's arrival, given that snakes do not seem especially popular around here. (The local attitude is perhaps best summed up by a resident of a snake-plagued Wilmington apartment complex, quoted in a recent story in the *Wilmington Star-News*: "I don't like those fellows with no shoulders.") But Dean has gotten no complaints from his neighbors — they're grateful for the business he brings to the area, he says — with the sole exception of a feline rescue organization whose members, he claims, are spreading a rumor that Dean stalks downtown alleys at dawn, collecting cats in a basket to feed to his snakes. ("Ludicrous," he tells me. "I never get up before 10 a.m.")

The Serpentarium snakes live in lush enclosures built to Dean's specifications by set designers from Screen Gems (Frank Capra Jr.'s Wilmington film studios), featuring stalactites and stalagmites and ropy roots and vines, real animal skulls and bones, moss-draped grottos and cypress knees and running waterfalls and ponds. Each snake is rated by a skull-and-bones icon to indicate its deadliness level (two skulls = life-threatening to children and the elderly, possible mild disfigurement; five skulls = survival unlikely), and plaques on the exhibits give detailed descriptions, extremely popular with children, of exactly how you will die if bitten by each particular snake.

Strolling through the Serpentarium I learn that the Egyptian cobra, whose festive yellow and black stripes remind me of Charlie Brown's shirt, was the "asp" that killed Cleopatra; in ancient Egypt, the plaque says, these snakes were awarded to royal prisoners as a means of suicide. The Asiatic spitting cobras, meanwhile, never seem to run out of venom, like "a sort of endless poisonous squirt gun." The bite of the Central American fer-de-lance, Dean attests, feels like having your hand slammed in a car door and then seared with a blowtorch. "The bitten extremity swells to massive proportions, the skin bursts open, and your eyes weep blood," the plaque helpfully elaborates.

The fifteen-foot king cobra, the longest venomous snake in the world, can kill an elephant with a single bite, and is known to rear up six feet in the air, hood flared, and look a man in the eye while growling like a dog. For some reason, perhaps a primal one, the male king cobra's eerie flat dirt color is scarier to me than some of the flashier patterns on display here. Likewise the look of the steely black mambas, who are long, skinny, and, according to their plaque, "excitable"—and indeed each time I've visited they were wide awake and slicing around their enclosure like gang members looking to get something started. Most disturbing of all, perhaps, are the fat puff adders, whose odd cigar-shaped bodies make them grotesquely evocative, like nightmare shape-shifter snakes. *We are snakes,* they seem to say, *but we are on the verge of becoming something else.*

The Serpentarium also exhibits a few nonvenomous reptiles, including a 250-pound python named Sheena, some ethereally beautiful emerald tree boas, and a nine-foot man-eating crocodile, which, like every crocodile, alligator, or lizard I've ever seen, looks disarmingly fake, motionless, prehistoric, and improbable. One day while I was visiting Dean, the girl at the front desk reported that a worried visitor claimed the beaded lizard looked dead. "It always looks dead," Dean said irritably. "That's how it looks." We went to check on the lizard, which was fine. It resembled a large, expensive purse. The plaque on its exhibit noted, "These lizards make excellent—if unresponsive—pets."

For sale in the Serpentarium lobby is a huge assortment of toy snakes, snake T-shirts and snake stickers and snake books, Viper Blast spray candy and Viper gum (and, inexplicably, Skittles), watercolor paintings by Dean's mother, carved Peruvian rainsticks, and a display of traditional African art and sculpture, available for purchase from a local importer. A sign on the front desk warns against tapping on the snakes' enclosures: *If you knew that the only thing standing between you and death was a pane of glass, would you risk breaking it?*

This is not P.T.–Barnum–style hyperbole. One day I was taking flash photos of an apparently pissed-off cobra (she was waving menacingly about, hood flared), my face as close as my camera lens would allow, when she finally had enough and struck at me, hitting the glass a centimeter from my eye. I had the delayed jolt you get right after a fender bender—*did that just really happen?*

Weekend feedings are even more shocking (and, again, beloved by children), especially for those expecting the type of theater you get at Sea World. Here there are literally no barriers. A few comically symbolic plastic yellow chains are hooked up to keep people out of the way, the enclosures propped open so nothing but air separates the poisonous snakes from the audience, and then Dean, or his curator, Scott, uses barbecue tongs to deliver the dead rats, jiggling them to get the snakes to strike, even climbing in with the snakes to prevent fights. (One might imagine the feeders wear something like astronaut suits, but the day I saw Dean break up a squabble between two bushmasters he was wearing a polo shirt and cargo shorts.) The yellow chains are, it turns out, unnecessary—men the size of line-backers dart to the back of the crowd, pretending they're just joking: *Ha-ha, I think I'll stand back here.* Some people can't even bear the sight of the feed-ers handing each other the dead rodents. "He's touching that rat like it ain't nothing," a woman murmurs.

People who devote their careers to animals—veterinarians, zoolo-gists—are often quite different in temperament from garden-variety animal lovers, taking a flat-footed, unsentimental approach to their subjects, maintaining a scientific skepticism of anthropomorphism. My mother worked as a docent at Chicago's Lincoln Park Zoo for twenty-five years and has an enormous collection of butterflies she traveled all over the world to catch, and my father is a life-long birdwatcher, getting up before dawn every weekend to search for rare shorebirds at landfills and sewerage plants. And yet neither of my parents is particularly roman-tic about the animals they love. They love them for perplexingly literal reasons—because they're such fascinating examples of evolution, or because they have "unusual plumage." My parents do not seem especially interested in talking or thinking about what animals are *like,* what they evoke or suggest, what they *mean*—all the things that are most interesting to me, the fiction writer in the family.

My favorite novelist, Joy Williams, once said in an interview that the Bible had influenced her "because all those wonderful stories—about snakes and serpents and mysterious seeds and trees—didn't mean what they seemed. They meant some other thing." In Williams's short story "Lu-Lu," the characters do nothing *but* sit around discussing the meaning of a giant snake (Lu-Lu) —whether she has a soul, how she seems to materialize and dematerialize at will, how she can occupy herself doing nothing. The snake continues to accrue symbolic weight until the story finally ends, hauntingly, with a young woman trying to coax the stoic Lu-Lu into her car: *How do you beckon to something like this, she wondered; something that can change everything, your life.* When I was twelve, my mother gave my father a pet boa constrictor for their anniversary, and never once in all the subsequent years we owned Jaws (we got and named her in 1978) did it occur to me that she could change *anything,* let alone our lives. We did not discuss her symbolism. We talked about whether she was going to shed her skin soon, or whether she was ready to move up from mice to rats.

So even before I meet Dean Ripa, I think I know what kind of person he will be. Though he has no advanced degree (he quit high school shortly before graduation, "for dramatic effect," he says), his snake collection is internationally recognized, his research on bushmasters published in herpetological journals. He is a scientist.

Then he gives me a copy of his essay, "Confessions of a Gaboon Viper Lover," which appeared in Gary Indiana's 1994 anthology *Living with the Animals.* It is a paean to Ripa's own late Gaboon viper, Madame Zsa Zsa. "Morphologically, she seems halfway to some unspeakable transformation that may or may not include a human head," he writes. Her pattern might have been lifted from a Persian carpet, he says, and also suggests skeletons. "One can *see* into the pattern," a Tanzanian witch priest told Dean, but then declined to say what it was he saw. The snake's design brings to mind "Kandinsky zigzags," the "meretricious skulls" of Georgia O'Keefe; its face suggests Bosch, or Dürer's engraving of the Devil in the Garden. "Like Dali's paranoiac-critical method of seeing the hidden face," Dean writes, "seeing the Gaboon viper seems largely participatory, on a parallel with perception itself." Watching a Gaboon viper "literally materialize before you from the debris of the forest floor," he concludes, "is perhaps the closest one can ever come among live creatures to the fright of encountering an actual ghost."

I notice that I am feeling slightly in love.

"It's definitely *not* like TV," Dean says, somewhat defiantly, about the Serpentarium experience. In fact Dean has been invited by various animal-related TV programs to bring his snakes out into the jungle, set them loose, and then pretend to discover them on camera, and he declines all such invitations on principle. In the wild, he says, snakes are nearly impossible to find — you will go years without finding the one you want, unless, like him, you know where to look.

He is telling me this in his apartment, whose entrance is an unmarked door on the Serpentarium's second level; he lives alone with his tiny nine-year-old Maltese dog, Wednesday (whom he also calls, variously, "Winky" and "Pinky"), and a couple aquariums full of deadly bushmasters in his bedroom. He has been married and divorced three times but claims his snakes played no part in his romantic misfortunes. "I'm just not somebody who can be halved," he says, enigmatically. I suggest that it must be hard to find women who will sleep in a room with snakes — or maybe some women think it's a turn-on? "You get both kinds," Dean says. Either way, it occurs to me, if one were going to sleep with Dean Ripa, one would have to have a great deal of faith in Dean Ripa.

Not long after he quit high school, Dean moved to Italy to study painting under portraitist Pietro Annigoni, whose work he had discovered in an art magazine. For a number of years, then, collecting and selling snakes became secondary, a way to support his art career. He enjoyed considerable success, spending time with Salvador Dali and selling two paintings to writer William S. Burroughs (these now hang on the walls of Dean's apartment, on loan from the Burroughs estate). His style is blackly surreal — muddy-hued portraits and still-lifes with hidden messages, faces, and severed limbs floating to their dark, dreamy surfaces. *Ripa's painting depicts biologic fragmentation,* Burroughs wrote. *The artist is giving birth to his selves on canvas.* I think of *Rosemary's Baby,* the paintings Mia Farrow sees on the corridor walls as she's being carried into her satanic neighbors' apartment, and I ask Dean why he so admired Annigoni, a more traditional, Renaissance-inspired realist. "I wanted to learn the secrets of the Old Masters," he says. "I've always been on a quest for hidden things, occult things. It's like the snakes. Certain things, to me, always seemed to promise more than they outwardly were."

In 1975, when Dean was eighteen, he sent William S. Burroughs the manuscript of a children's book he was writing called *Johnny Zimb.* He didn't know Burroughs but was a devoted fan of his work, its renegade exoticism seeming to speak directly to the "voices in my head," he says. *Johnny Zimb*'s plot was "a scarecrow-boy type of thing" he tells me. "You know, a surrealistic thing." Burroughs replied to Dean, *I think you have written a very good children's book, though perhaps a little too complex and literate for juvenile reading.* Over the years that followed, their correspondence and friendship escalated, Burroughs sending letters to Dean in Ecuador, Ghana, Surinam, and Costa Rica, giving advice on writing and asking Dean's advice on painting, inviting him to visit at his home in Lawrence, Kansas. They exchanged knives, guns, snakes, and, at one point, a human skull Dean claimed to have robbed from a grave as a teenager. (*I did indeed receive Helen with open arms,* Burroughs wrote in thanks. *I know how difficult it was for you to part with her.*) One time Dean brought Burroughs a suitcase full of snakes; another time he set a cobra loose in Burroughs's living room. While I'm reading through their letters, Dean goes into his room and brings out a

.357 Magnum that Burroughs gave him, mentioning offhandedly as he sets it on the table before me that it's loaded. (*Jesus*, I think, *how many different things that can kill you can one person keep in his bedroom?*)

Burroughs's letters to Dean are full of fond and cryptic personal counsel: *Oh and as for Madame Whosit and her Oath of Secrecy I would caution you to stay well away from her dubious emanations. She sounds like bad news.* In the mid-Eighties, Burroughs asked Dean to write a letter about centipede venom that he could include in his novel, *The Western Lands*; it appears in the text unedited, and Dean is thanked in the book's acknowledgments. *Have you thought of writing your memoirs as a snake catcher?* Burroughs wrote Dean in 1986. *I have just finished a cat book.* And again in 1988, Burroughs suggested, *Why not write a book about your experiences as a snake catcher? Your letters to me would be a good start.* Then, as now, however, Dean was more interested in writing fiction and collecting snakes.

When Burroughs died of heart failure in 1997, Dean was at his bedside; he happened to be visiting that month ("I don't think it was a coincidence," he tells me). He had never seen someone die before, and he stayed at Burroughs's house for days afterward, even sleeping in his bed, while fans came and went, leaving flowers at the door.

Nowadays, in between endless interruptions from the Serpentarium downstairs, Dean is working on a couple of novels, at least parts of which are based on his own experiences. He shows me the thick manuscript of one, *Succumbu (Mama Sleep)*, but then will only let me read its first line: *The beauty of Hell is that it is self-regenerating.*

It is impossible to meet Dean Ripa and not think of John Laroche, the eccentric outlaw orchid breeder Susan Orlean wrote about in *The Orchid Thief* (played by Chris Cooper so brilliantly in the film version, *Adaptation*). But while the orchid thief's passions and obsessions "arrived unannounced and ended explosively, like car bombs" (he had already abandoned orchids by the time Orlean finished writing about him), Dean's loves—painting, writing, and most especially snakes—seem eternal. "I'm doing the exact same things now that I was doing when I was ten years old," he says.

Dean dreams about snakes all the time. Sometimes they are good dreams: that he discovers he owns snakes he didn't know about, that aliens abduct him and take him to a secret part of North Carolina that was incompletely glaciated (there is always a scientific explanation, even in Dean's dreams), revealing a colony of rare snakes. He also has nightmares that his snakes are dying, that they're eating each other, that he forgot to feed them, that he must protect them from some unseen danger. He almost never dreams that his snakes bite or kill him; it is always the snakes that are in jeopardy, that he must save.

"The greater the value of a collection, the greater the risk of loss that it represents," Philipp Blom writes in *To Have and to Hold: An Intimate History of Collectors and Collecting*. To collect is to continually negotiate with the afterlife, with the fact that *you can't take it with you*. Even worse, if you collect living things you must also confront their mortality. In *The Orchid Thief*, Susan Orlean calls collecting "a sort of love sickness." Because orchids die, "to desire orchids," Orlean says, "is to have a desire that will never be, can never be, fully requited." So what kind of person devotes his life to collecting something both mortal *and* deadly? A collection that is both hard to keep alive and that might at any moment kill you?

Dean has ten times endured the bites of potentially lethal snakes (including the cottonmouth when he was fourteen), yet he insists his romance has always been with danger, not death—"like St. George and the dragon," he says. *It was some Greek said that men give themselves more trouble than is ordained by the Gods*, Burroughs wrote to Dean in 1989. *A parish priest would tell you that your trouble is scruples. Like . . . you make things more complicated than they need to be and more categorical. . . . So take things philosophic and remember you have reached a point where antivenom is almost more dangerous than snakebite.* Dean claims Burroughs meant this last comment literally, since antivenom really can be as deadly as the snakebite itself. Still, it strikes me as beautiful, Zen-like advice.

I ask whether he suffers lingering effects from the envenomings. "I don't know about lingering effects, but I don't feel so great," he says and laughs weakly, like he's not exactly joking. He claims he has a headache and I offer him something—I've got every kind of painkiller in my purse, I tell him, thanks to a recent dental procedure. "Well, then you'll lead a long life," he says wearily. He does admit he's more easily fatigued these days, but that might be a result of the malaria, schistosomiasis, dysentery, and miscellaneous other tropical ailments he contracted during his travels. His hands are weaker from the bites, he says, and he has a greater tolerance for pain. Also, he fears death less than he used to, but this is not necessarily a good thing. "Actually what scares me isn't death," he clarifies, "but that I'll forget to fear death." He doesn't mean this figuratively or philosophically—he means: during feeding times.

Religious snake handlers sometimes try to buy snakes from Dean, but he won't sell to them, claiming his snakes are just too deadly ("They don't have enough faith for my snakes, believe me," he says). Yet he has no objection to what the handlers do and even declares, "If I had a religion, that would probably be it. At least they're willing to test, to prove what they believe." He adds, "Actually I might be a magic animist, if I'm anything. I'm interested in voodoo, but I would never call myself a voodooist. I don't like organized things, groups, mobs. The most frightening thing in the world is a group of people standing there."

When too many visitors pack the Serpentarium, Dean hides out in his apartment. But, I say, I thought your purpose with the Serpentarium was to educate people. "I'm not here to educate people," he says. "I couldn't give a damn what happens to them." But then he adds, grudgingly, "Well, there are some people worth something, and ideally they'd get something out of it." By now I've grown accustomed (and rather devoted) to Dean's rhetorical style—*outrageous overstatement, subsequent qualification*—but I think I recognize something else, something authentic here: a certain strain of introverted misanthropy that often leads people to commit their lives to animals, something I think I know about from my family. Introverts and loners love animals. It runs the spectrum, I think, from my father's boyhood shyness to the full-fledged autism of Temple Grandin—and it's a trait I find familiar and strangely comforting.

It's Friday night in Wilmington and I'm at Alleigh's, a brightly horrifying "entertainment complex," featuring a warehouse-sized, earsplitting arcade, but I'm in a low-lit back room, watching the allegedly hermitic Dean Ripa perform astonishingly lovely renditions of Sinatra romantic standards before a delighted, dressed-up crowd of about a hundred, backed by a seventeen-piece orchestra that has come from miles away for this gig (out-of-state license plates in the parking lot say *SAXAFON* and *STRAUSS*). Dean organized the entire evening himself, sorting musical arrangements, assembling band members, advertising with flyers in the Serpentarium lobby: *Come hear DEAN RIPA, "THE VOICE," singing Sinatra, Bobby Darin & other favorites from years gone by! MONSTER ENTERTAINMENT!!*

I feel disoriented, like I've crashed someone's wedding in 1963. Dean does "Mack the Knife," "Fly Me to the Moon," "The Best Is Yet to Come." He dances with the microphone, he gets down on one knee, he keeps up a mild, unintrusive patter with the audience in between songs. He does "I've Got You Under My Skin," "Witchcraft," "Come Fly With Me." During "New York, New York," three tipsy middle-aged women spontaneously join him on the dance floor, kick off their shoes, and do a can-can, cheered on by the crowd. There is no sign or mention anywhere of snakes.

My friends and I came expecting Vegas-style camp (and in fact a poster at the entrance advertises an upcoming Elvis impersonator's show) but Dean's performance is sincere, his delivery charged and charming (but not cheesy), his voice accomplished and smooth. He's not making fun of Sinatra, nor trying to be Sinatra. He's just singing. He's so good I doubt my own ears and double-check with my friends—maybe it's the Percocet?—but no, they're equally enthused. None of us can shake the odd, giddy feeling that we've stepped into an alternate dimension, a parallel Wilmington. Where did all these people *come* from? Who *is* Dean Ripa, anyway?

After the show I breathlessly compliment him on his performance, then worry I'm insulting him by sounding so surprised. I thought it was going to be like Lawrence Welk, I say. "What you need to know about me," he says, "is that Lawrence Welk is my archenemy." He does not elaborate.

Well, so, what *is* all this? I ask. A hobby?

"I don't have hobbies," Dean says. "Everything I do is work." In fact, a few months after this show, he will be hired on as the lead vocalist with the Tommy Dorsey Orchestra and go on the road throughout the South, getting rave reviews — *A handsome hunk with a voice to match . . . abducted the audience from their mundane existences . . . dares us to experience ecstasy again!* For the moment, he allows that his snakes don't provide quite the same adrenaline they used to, that these days he finds a live audience scarier and hence more thrilling than the possibility of death by snakebite. Like his hero Sinatra, Dean has never learned to read music, because, he says, "it was too boring." I recall what he told me about his brief stint in the Peace Corps, teaching industrial arts in Liberian villages on the eve of a bloody coup in which the country's president was overthrown: "It was the boringest thing you could imagine." He left long before his assignment was over. "I could never complete a job or do anything anyone told me to, never take orders from anyone," he says, then adds sheepishly, and unconvincingly, "except people I love."

A few days later I'm sitting on Dean's living room floor, a sudden downpour roaring onto the tin roofs outside, before me on the coffee table a clutter of art books and herpetology journals, as well as a luminescent dead dragonfly Dean found on his balcony and dropped absently into my palm while pacing around the room answering my questions. It occurs to me to ask if he is a Scorpio, or perhaps born in the Chinese Year of the Snake. No, he says — but then it turns out *we have the same birthday*. I feel like I might have a heart attack. Dean goes on a fierce hunt for his birth certificate, because what if we were also born *at the same time!* He drags out files and manila envelopes but finally gives up. (He finds it a few days later: We were born a couple hours, not to mention nine years, apart. So what, he says, they could have made a mistake—were they holding a stopwatch or what?) When I manage to breathe again, I quiz Dean about Capricorn traits: stubborn (check), obsessive (check), respect for the traditional (check). "I have a lot of respect for tradition," he says, "even though I'm constantly trying to smash it."

Not long after this, I'm zipping down Eastwood Road, the busy four-lane highway that leads to Wrightsville Beach, when, improbably, I see a little box turtle attempting to cross right in my path: I will be the one to kill him. Without even deliberating I brake and put on my blinkers, a column of angry drivers backing up behind me, grab the turtle and run down the embankment to deposit him safely by a pond at the edge of somebody's yard—*and there's an alligator sitting there.* (I set the turtle down *away* from the alligator.) I get an incredible rush, the wild overpowering urge to leave my car idling with its door open in the middle of the road and just keep walking, keep going, because surely right around the bend lies something even bigger, just waiting for me. It's like I'm being handed some exhilarating responsibility I can't begin to name. "Once you make that bargain," I recall Dean telling me one day, apropos of nothing as we drove along in his truck, "the assignments start coming faster and faster." He might have been talking about snakes, art, life—he never said. But right now I'm sure I know what he meant.

WENDY BRENNER is the author of two story collections, *Phone Calls from the Dead* and *Large Animals in Everyday Life*, which won the Flannery O'Connor Award. Her stories and essays have appeared in numerous magazines and anthologies including *The Best American Essays, Best American Magazine Writing,* and *New Stories from the South*. She is a contributing editor for *Oxford American* magazine and teaches writing in the MFA program at the University of North Carolina at Wilmington.

The Face of the River

VIRGINIA HOLMAN

ONE RECENT FRIDAY AFTERNOON, I poached Kemp Burdette from his day job for a sunny day of john-boating on the Northeast Cape Fear River. Kemp is the Cape Fear River Keeper. You have likely seen him on television or all over your Facebook feed. He's a fit, tan man with close-cropped silvering hair. He's not quite young enough to call young and not quite old enough to call youthful. He's at the top of the hill, as my neighbor likes to say of those not firmly in middle age.

Kemp should be on top of the world. He's newly famous. Rachel Maddow discovered him shortly after he and a group of other River Keepers released a shocking video of deliberate coal ash dumping in the Cape Fear River. Coming on the heels of the Dan River coal ash disaster, the footage that aired on television went viral, and Kemp was thrust into the national spotlight. Suddenly the entire world knew what many of us in the area have known for years—that in the coastal plain of North Carolina much of our drinking water comes from the Cape Fear River and its tributaries, and that men like Kemp Burdette and organizations like Cape Fear River Watch are at the forefront of protecting the public health.

I've met a few River Keepers in my day, and in my experience, they are not flashy people with out out-of-control egos. In aggregate, River Keepers are understated, smart enough not to let on just how frighteningly smart they are, pit-bull tenacious, and relentlessly driven. River Keepers know the history of the communities they protect and they are personally acquainted with those who make their living from the water. So far as I can tell, being a River Keeper is akin to being both environmental sheriff and good ol' boy. River Keepers don't carry badges, and I'm fairly certain they aren't issued a sidearm. But if one takes you out on the Northeast Cape Fear in his johnboat, you can bet he's brought two essential pieces of equipment: a machete and a laptop computer.

You might think that scheduling face time with a famous River Keeper requires a have-your-people-call-my-people sort of arrangement. When I call to discuss a story about the Northeast Cape Fear River, Kemp kindly offers to explore the river with me. So much for fame going to his head. Then he says four words that every wilderness freak longs to hear: *black bears, bobcats,* and *bucks.*

In 2013, Cape Fear River Watch, in conjunction with the North Carolina Coastal Federation and the Wildlands Network, received a $35,000 grant from wildlife conservationists Brad and Shelli Stanback to install and maintain twenty-four infrared wildlife cameras along the waterway. Most of the cameras are installed in areas only accessible by boat, and all are so well concealed they are impossible to spot, even up close. "I am amazed by the images we've captured so far," says Kemp. "Bobcat especially. I've been fishing, camping, and hunting in this area since I was a boy, and I have never ever seen a bobcat in the wild. But with the cameras, we've seen dozens out here."

Kemp and I head upriver from the Castle Hayne public boat ramp. We pass beneath a bridge, and within minutes the river corridor appears mostly uninhabited and wild, save for the looming towers from an old cement plant. Most people in the area are more familiar with the Cape Fear River than its tributary, the sensibly named Northeast Cape Fear River, known locally as "East Branch." The Northeast Cape Fear's headwaters rise in Duplin County, near Mount Olive. From there this blackwater waterway slides past the primevally beautiful Goshen Swamp, Angola Bay, Holly Shelter Game Land, and through the rural community of Castle Hayne. It joins the Cape Fear River north of downtown. More than likely you've simply noted this river as a landmark—it's the last waterway you cross on I-40 South as you enter Wilmington. This elegant riparian corridor extends nearly one hundred and thirty miles through bottomland hardwoods and cypress gum swamps, and alongside pristine upland forest.

Longtime North Carolina residents who follow the news know the Northeast Cape Fear has suffered mightily from industrial pollution over the last forty years—everything from hog waste to hydraulic fluid to oil and mercury have tainted the river. In addition, some of the aquifer near its banks in Castle Hayne has been polluted since the mid-1970s by a massive hexavalent chromium plume. (You may recognize the name—hexavalent chromium is the same carcinogen featured in the film *Erin Brockovich*.) This leak has poisoned the groundwater in the spill area. Since groundwater moves, the plume is kept in check by an elaborate system of wells and pumps, and will be in perpetuity. And you'd have to have been living under a rock to have missed the contentious, years-long debate about locating Titan America's proposed cement plant along its riverbanks.

If you only know about the Northeast Cape Fear from the news, you might think it is a place of limited value as wilderness. Or that it's a place not worth visiting, not worth saving. Despite its checkered past and uncertain future, the Northeast Cape Fear is one of the most stunning wild areas that you can visit in the Wilmington metro area. North Carolina's Department of Environment and Natural Resources (NCDENR) heartily agrees. That's why the area has been designated a nationally significant natural heritage area by its North Carolina Natural Heritage Program. NCDENR realizes this area is an important nursery site for anadromous fish, and it's also home to federally endangered shortnose sturgeon and red-cockaded woodpeckers. In addition, the area has several federal species of concern including Rafinesque's big-eared bat and yellow lampmussel.

Yet conservation-minded organizations like Cape Fear River Watch know it's hard to get folks excited about protecting the river by making the humble yellow lampmussel the "face of the river." If Kemp had suggested we hit the river so he could show me shellfish, I would have smiled politely and told him I'd get back to him once I'd checked my calendar. Offer to show me black bear cubs and bobcat, and I am ready to roll. Kemp's familiar with this reaction. People want to see these splendid creatures. When they do, they remember, and they want to help protect their habitat here on the river.

As Kemp and I motor up the river, it's evident that the Northeast Cape Fear is what makes Castle Hayne a truly special place. Spring is in full swing. A golden sheen of pollen lines the banks, and down several creeks I can see the waterlilies beginning to bud. A small orchid has sprouted on a decaying tree limb. Two ospreys have returned to nest in a large cypress, and the male swoops back to the nest to check on his mate, a red shiner writhing in his talons.

Kemp guides our boat to shore in a heavily forested area to retrieve data from one of the hidden wildlife cameras. A fat water snake is coiled on a low hanging branch, and it's so bold as to not be disturbed by our presence until we are two feet away. On shore, Kemp unlocks the secure cage where the camera is kept and then quickly draws back his hand. "This happens a lot." The box is swarming with fire ants.

"We get wasps too." He shakes off the camera, extracts the memory card, and downloads the photos onto his computer. This camera has recorded well over two hundred photos. I'm amazed at what's passed through here in the preceding couple of weeks: wild turkeys, bears, otters, a lone blue heron, and numerous deer. The variety of wildlife is astonishing, even more so when I consider that the area captured by the cameras is relatively small, not much more than fifty square feet.

The wildlife cameras are set not to detect motion, but heat. Once heat is detected, they take a photo a second. The result at times is a beautiful, fractured, slow-motion series. Some images—a buck swimming across a creek at night, two black bears roving the understory at dawn—are as elegant and haunting as anything you'd see at an art gallery. Other images of wildlife in action—a black bear scratching its back on a tree or a blue heron giving the camera box the eye—are hilarious. The daytime photos are in color, and the nighttime photos in black and white. An infrared flash provides enough light to take the photo but not so much that it scares off the animals. Occasionally, a shot will show an inquisitive deer or coyote staring directly at the camera, likely because, unlike humans, they can smell it or hear its tiny motor.

We visit a couple of other sites and inspect the photos. A shot of a doe shows three shining sets of eyes in the distance. The height makes Kemp think they're coyotes.

A powerful bobcat slinks past in another frame. A family of deer is digitally captured, and they move along in a nocturnal ballet, until one takes a bathroom break. "I see a lot of that with the deer," he laughs. He downloads more photos onto his laptop, secures the camera, and conceals it with some brush he's gathered with his machete. Once again, it's invisible.

Before we wrap up for the day, I ask him to head down nearby Island Creek, one of my favorite spots to kayak. This sheltered creek is shaded by a beautiful forest canopy, and punctuated by massive old-growth cypress trees. It's also one of the best sites I know for seeing the vivid yellow prothonotary warblers. Two beaver lodges have been recently constructed on the southern shore, and I hear a hawk keen.

Kemp asks the time, and it breaks my heart to depart from such a lovely place, but I know the shy inhabitants of the river forest are waiting patiently for us to leave.

VIRGINIA HOLMAN writes the Excursions column for *Salt* magazine. Her work has been reprinted in the Pushcart Prize Series, broadcast on *This American Life,* and was a B&N Great New Authors selection. She has received fellowships and awards from the North Carolina Arts Council and the Carter Center, and has taught at UNC-Chapel Hill and UNC Wilmington. An outdoorsy type, she also occasionally serves as a kayak guide.

The Sea Is a Collector

JEAN JONES

Tell me, Scott, when the woman stopped singing,
and night descended, and you and I walked back to town,
beyond the beach as the sun sunk down toward the distant west,
why, as we stood out waiting for approaching night,
did we not say anything to one another?
You finally asked, "What is the sea?"
and I said, "The sea is a collector,"
and as we stood and watched the shrimping boats, out in the distance,
laying out and pulling in their nets with Venus and the night stars
    coming out,
one by one, with the roar of the sea constant in our ears,
the tide receding out, the shells by our feet, and the woman,
walking away in the distance, I kept wanting to ask you,
"What is the sea, Scott? Why do you want to know?"
But you said nothing.

Originally from Indonesia, **JEAN JONES** teaches basic skills English as a Second Language at Cape Fear Community College in Wilmington. He has published two books of poetry with St. Andrews Press: *Birds of Djakarta* and *Invocations of Mystery*.

Street Scenes

Ballads of Change

ASHLEY WAHL

SEEMS LIKE A LIFETIME has passed since that third-floor apartment on the outskirts of Greensboro's tony Fisher Park—potted herbs struggling on the rickety fire escape, cockroaches scuttling inside 1950s walls thin as Bible pages.

It was oddly charming, that one-bedroom space I called home while writing stories for a magazine whose famous namesake, O. Henry, was born there but penned his stories elsewhere. I knew, however, that Greensboro was a temporary address for me.

Two years ago, when I got a chance to move to Wilmington to help launch *Salt,* a storytelling magazine that celebrates the art and soul of this Port City, I was ready for a new adventure. We set up shop on Front Street in historic downtown, where I began to observe the distinct rhythm of a place that has no doubt experienced its fair share of change. And then we moved again, to a new office up ever-bustling Market Street.

This is Wilmington as I see it. A tale of one city from two views.

Front Street is a poem I know by heart.

Beyond the walls of the old Bullock Hospital Building, the world gained momentum with each cup of coffee. Neighbors became friends, and you could set your watch to the daily routines of perfect strangers, like the woman with the wire-haired terrier, always at the Bijou Park courtyard at eight o'clock, always smiling in the dappled morning light.

Time itself moved at a different speed. Days clicked by like carriage horses. They were peppered with snippets of conversations from tourists and ghost walk tours; punctuated by fiery sunsets over the glimmering Cape Fear.

No sooner had I grown accustomed to the pace and patter of Front Street than the *Salt* offices moved to "The Switchyard" off Market Street, a funky industrial space laced with railroad spur that interrupts nature. The drive here takes you past a dense stand of towering pines and a small pond, bluebirds and buntings springing forth like bits of confetti as resident dogs roam the grassy lot off-leash. It's a curious hideaway: Walden Pond smack in between Bojangles' Famous Chicken 'n Biscuits and the Carmike 16 Cinema.

Here at the former site of a power boat facility (before that it was a fertilizer distribution center), birds run on a schedule set more by the seasons than the clock. Like the small blue heron, who fishes at twilight. Or the belted kingfisher, silent on his low-level perch. Or the snowy egret, wading through the shallows as if on stilts.

The raucous call of the red-headed woodpecker carries through wind and glass. You can watch him from the loft, flitting between two hollow pines beyond the tracks: back and forth, back and forth, tucking away extra grub for later.

Like an ancient goddess, the sycamore reveals the beauty of each season. Her meters are varied but her rhythm you can't deny.

Wilmington artist Claude Howell was working as a stenographer at the Atlantic Coast Line Railroad when he witnessed the 1936 demolition of the old downtown post office building. He wrote about it in his sacred journal:

> It is rather sad, watching the brown sandstone wall crumbling down bit by bit. . . . I always took the building for granted, but now that it is going I feel like I am losing an old friend.

That's how it felt to discover that the lot beside the Wetsig pond was being cleared last fall.

As the last tree crashed into the earth, I mourned for the birds.

From the windowed loft, a beam of light, a thin veil of pine fringes the pond, beyond which Wilmington's newest fire station slowly rises. The crew works rhythmically, the droning of construction machinery adding to the ever-expanding ballad.

Weeks pass, but the familiars return. First, heron and egret. Then, belted kingfisher. Turtles re-emerge, parking like cars along the sunny bank, but no woodpecker. Not for a while.

Shortly after the woodpecker's return, welcome as a smile from the art council's Rhonda Bellamy on a walk to the downtown post office, the blustering winds of an early spring rain felled one of the hollow pines. I was looking out the window when it snapped in two.

Day after the storm, a raucous call announced the woodpecker was back—again. From my perch, I watched him flit between the dead pine that weathered the storm and a tall, healthy-looking pine. In nature, there's no time to mourn. He works rhythmically, raps on a new door.

Change is the poem he knows by heart.

ASHLEY WAHL grew up in the North Carolina Sandhills, just six miles from the Weymouth Center in Southern Pines. After graduating from the University of North Carolina at Greensboro in 2009, she moved back to her hometown and began writing for *The Pilot* newspaper and its award-winning *PineStraw* magazine. In 2011, when *The Pilot* launched *O.Henry* magazine in Greensboro, she served as associate editor until relocating to Wilmington in 2013. She now is the senior editor of *Salt* magazine, a sister publication of *O.Henry* and *PineStraw*.

Gather 'Round the Table

JASON FRYE

A CLOUD OF STEAM erupts from the pot of oysters. Made double by the chill November afternoon, it hangs in the air like some great saline thunderhead in miniature before dissipating.

Our oyster master pulls the basket and gives it a cursory shake before upending it, sending the half bushel of oysters clattering onto a newspaper-covered picnic table. Someone reaches in, rakes the pile smooth, spreading the rocky pile around the table. I grab one, and immediately regret my haste. Rather than shuck it, I toss it from hand to hand until it's cool enough to eat. A couple of my companions follow suit.

We have all the trappings to put down another bushel: three sleeves of Saltines; two coffee mugs of butter someone cleverly balanced on the lid of the steam pot to melt; a pair of hot sauces — Texas Pete and Cholula; seven oyster knives (no one knows where number eight disappeared to).

Gathering around a mess of oysters — or better yet, a couple of pecks buried beneath layers of soaking wet burlap, roasting away on a slab of corrugated tin suspended over an open fire — is a Southern food tradition. Like barbecue or a full-blown pig pickin', we here in North Carolina like to think we invented these food-centered gatherings. But we didn't. We just perfected them. Stop anywhere along the coast from Florida to Maine and you'll find similar gatherings, except the oysters may be replaced by whatever's local: stone crabs or blue crabs or clams or lobster. Follow the coast and you'll find subtle variations in traditional dishes and communal dining.

Growing up in the coalfields of southern West Virginia, I knew food traditions that were decidedly different. Gathering around a plate of food meant a church potluck, Decoration Day—that's Memorial Day for the ones holding to the old ways—at the family cemetery, reunions, coal-camp gatherings, a holiday cookout with my grandparents. In spring, we'd eat morels and ramps and bowls of wild greens—creasy, poke, dandelion— most often served wilted under hot bacon grease my grandmother had saved and beside cornbread she made in the cast-iron skillet that's now my sister's. In summers, it was farm-to-table dining, gathering our vegetables from my grandfather's garden an hour or two before mealtime. Fall meant hunting and stewpots full of squirrel and grouse. Winter was for whatever you'd canned that summer.

When I moved to Wilmington, I came to a place where I had to learn new foodways. There was no cemetery to visit for Decoration Day, no grandmother's yard in which to have a cookout, no mountain to forage with my grandfather. In many ways, I had arrived in a foreign land.

Not to say that North Carolina or her shore were foreign. We'd visited frequently—the Outer Banks, Wrightsville, other beach areas where I fell in love with North Carolina seafood.

Cooking seafood was unchartered waters for us mountain folk who avoided the fishmonger where the tuna was not sold by the can and where sardines were baitfish. During one beach vacation, my uncle and I caught a bucketful of flounder, which was subsequently knocked over by high-washing surf, sending my aunt sprawling across a half dozen flounder as they fought their way back to the sea and she fought in vain to save our dinner. We ended up trying to cook the few remaining fish, but it turned out we really didn't know how to cook them. We had to supplement supper that night with a pizza.

Mostly I ate my seafood at buffets at coastal restaurants. By my standards today, the food wasn't good, but you gotta start somewhere, and it was there my eyes were opened.

Which brings me back to that oyster roast.

Only two of the many gathered around the table in Wilmington are North Carolina natives, and only one of us hails from the coast. The rest of us are transplants. From the mountains. From Up North. From the West Coast, the Midwest, the Rust Belt. But we're all here now, putting down roots in soil strange to us, but it's become our soil all the same.

We've taken part in enough oyster roasts collectively and individually to understand the ritual. There's the preparation: Buy your oysters from Eagle Island (unless you "got a guy"), rinse them of marsh mud and sand and silt, keep them chilled and damp until it's time. The cooking: half a steamer basket at a time, reserve a few for those on-the-half-shell folks. The serving: With a utility-gloved or dishtowel-wrapped hand, lift the basket from the water and give it a shake; dump the whole thing onto a newspaper-lined table; provide hot sauce, crackers, and butter to taste.

Once the oysters are on the table, it's a free-for-all orgy, a beer-soaked bivalve bacchanal that ends up with someone burning their fingers on a too-hot oyster and someone else stabbing their hand with an oyster knife.

We manage well enough with the oyster knives, and after a few false starts, everyone is popping open the shells with a twist of the wrist. Though we think we're doing well, each and every one of us spits out a little piece of shell after every couple of oysters.

After eating a few, I clean off my knife blade and go for one of the raw ones, careful to open the shell in such a way that the liquor—the liquid locked inside with the oyster—is preserved. With a quick scrape along the cup, the oyster is loose and, a dash of hot sauce later, I slurp it down. A couple of other guys grab a cold, raw oyster and do the same.

Our experience with raw oysters runs the gamut from a ritzy New Years Eve party where they are served with champagne mignonette to grabbing one from an Inner Banks oyster bed and eating it as fresh and unadulterated as it can get. Most of us were introduced to raw oysters in our twenties or thirties, some of us drawn by the mythical aphrodisiac qualities they're said to possess, others by way of expanding our food universe. No matter how we got to the oyster table, we're caught in the moment, sharing bread and salt in the form of cracker and oyster, and taking part in the food culture of Wilmington.

We've eaten four or five on-the-half-shell and the neighbor's kid appears. He's six, maybe seven, and he bellies up to the table like it's the only place in this world where he belongs. Before any of the fathers in our group can say a word, he has grabbed an oyster knife in one hand and an oyster in the other.

"Little man, you need any . . ." one dad says.

The kid shakes his head, his too-blond, too-long mane waggles "no." Then, with a practiced precision none of us can fathom, he presses the point of the knife, angles the blade a little, gives a twist, and pops the oyster open. He eats it, shucks another, eats that, and one more. Then he's off, plunging into the fray of kids on the other side of the yard.

This kid gives me hope. At his age, to have developed a taste for oysters, to be so adept with the oyster knife, and to feel he can sidle up to a table of men says a lot about who he is. It reflects well on his past, present, and future, and the future of Wilmington. If he's this confident, this open now, where will he be at sixteen? At twenty-six? When his own son is six?

Someplace good. That place is here. He's already on his way to holding fast to the traditions of oyster roasts and other indigenous dishes— Christmas flounder and collard greens and grits and all the food that is holy in the South. He is here in Wilmington carrying its food traditions into the next generation.

JASON FRYE has explored every corner of the state as a food and travel writer, but he always returns home to Wilmington. The author of three travel guides—*Moon North Carolina, Moon North Carolina Coast including the Outer Banks,* and *Moon Road Trips: Blue Ridge Parkway*— and countless articles for *Our State, Salt,* the *Star-News,* he finds time and again he writes about the place and people he loves.

Beer Is Love

EVERYBODY GOES TO THE FAT PELICAN for the beer.

Hell, the bar's motto is "Beer is love," but the drinks are probably the least interesting part of the best dive bar in North Carolina. I remember my first time at the Carolina Beach landmark. It was summer and I was new to the area. Everyone I knew urged me to check out the place. I took a ride down to Carolina Beach on a warm night and found the bar on South Lake Park Boulevard. It was hard to miss the massive green moose near the front door.

Inside I noticed the refrigerated truck trailer attached to the bar. Purchased for $2,000 by the Fat Pelican's orginal owner, it houses one of the deepest beer selections in the Cape Fear area. The first time you peel back the plastic curtain can be overwhelming, as you walk into rows and rows of bottles and cans of beer. Stocked with over 400 different varieties, it caters to the beer snobs and drinkers of Miller Lite and Bud Heavy and everything in between. All the bartender does is pop the top and collect the money. There are no chemistry drinks at the Fat Pelican.

With a beer in hand, it is then impossible not to get sucked into the decor. The cramped bar area is decorated with all manner of Christmas lights, neon, and knickknacks. Hanging over the bar is a pair of size 22 white basketball shoes once owned by Shaquille O'Neal. Owner Danny McLaughlin traded a *Starsky & Hutch* model car for them, or so he says. The shoes are among hundreds of mementoes crammed into every corner, each one with its own story.

Wilmington has its share of bars with personality, but few can top the Fat Pelican. Danny isn't one to pass anything up, like Shaq's shoes over the bar, especially if it will keep people entertained.

"If you come in here, there is something to look at," Danny says as we walk around the bar on a cold winter morning. "Your eyes are occupied. It doesn't get stale. There is always something changing. If you keep the mind occupied, your body is going to hang around."

The bar opened in June 1986, built out of the remnants of a garage. Carolina Beach reminded Jim Kelly, the bar's first owner, of Key West. It started out as a beer and wine store, but in 1992, the liquor store next door left and Kelly decided to start selling drinks. When Danny took over a few years later, things started to get weird.

"I came here to create something," Danny says. "And I have. I've created the diviest dive bar in North Carolina."

A massive man with a thick beard and a mischievous glint in his eye, Danny is dressed in a denim jacket and a Fat Pelican hat pulled over his gray hair. He is cleaning up and getting the bar ready for the weekend crowd. He shows me a lamp made out of an anti-aircraft shell from the *USS Enterprise,* a World War II carrier. Danny found it at a yard sale in Connecticut for $5. A depth gauge from the Aquarius Reef Base, the world's only permanent undersea laboratory off the coast of Florida, hangs on a nail near the bar. It used to be manned by students from UNC Wilmington.

"Where did you get that?" I ask about the gauge.

"I knew the project manager," Danny says.

He doesn't explain how it came to hang in his bar, but it isn't hard to figure out.

As we walk around, you get a sense the bar was constructed from Carolina Beach's castoffs. Each room feels like it was built independently with material found around town and then stitched onto the bar. The floor is uneven and made of salvaged bricks or tile. Seating is eclectic with chairs and couches with mismatched cushions and even a dentist chair. Vintage video games take up one room near the bar.

Patrons keep a running dialogue and record of the bar on the walls. Except for the murals that cover two sides of the room, the rest of the bar's wall space is filled with graffiti—from names and dates scrawled with black marker to attempts at poetry. Outside, patrons sit on swings, in a wooden boat, or on the handmade wooden picnic tables or Adirondack chairs that rest in the sand. A Brahma bull on a surfboard watches over the outdoor seating.

135

"No bull man, I've got a bull," Danny says as we walk outside to look at it.

The bull sits on top of the workshop where Danny makes all of the bar's wooden furniture. Made of papier-mâché and foam, it was an advertisement for roast beef sandwiches at his friend's restaurant.

The bull is massive with black spots and long horns, with its head cocked looking over its shoulder at a black shark fin as it paddles a yellow surfboard. When the papier-mâché started to come apart, Danny's friend asked him to take it off the roof of a van used by the restaurant. Danny would only do it if he could have it for the bar.

"I put $450 worth of fiberglass on it and stuck it on top of the garage," Danny said. "The shark fin is the front end of a sailboat. We sawed it off.

"I now have a full-sized Brahma bull on a surfboard and he is looking back at the shark chasing him. It's hell when you have an imagination like mine."

It is easy to see where the imagination comes from. Danny's background is almost as colorful as his bar. Pre–Fat Pelican, he worked as a Maytag repairman, did explosive work on construction sites, served two tours in Vietnam with the First Cavalry Division where he was shot and survived a helicopter crash. But his most interesting job might have been when he started "Food 4 Sound," a catering business for rock bands.

Danny catered shows for everyone from Bruce Springsteen to Van Halen and Hank Williams Jr. The Police offered him a blank check to go on tour with them, but he had to turn down Sting and the boys because of other commitments.

Now, Danny is content to own the Fat Pelican. Unlike much of Carolina Beach, he stays open year-round even though he loses money in the winter. The way he sees it, the bar makes enough in the summer to cover the losses and his employees don't have to worry about losing their jobs. Plus, he prefers the local crowds who fill the place off-season.

"I got it made here," Danny says. "Hopefully I've got it set up so that when I'm dead and gone it will still be here. I'm sixty-five. I don't plan on living forever. I'm having too much fun."

And just to prove it, he leaves me with a joke. He tells me a friend in Washington, DC, gets him official White House golf balls. Then he leans in and delivers the punch line: "Don't tell no one I've been playing with the president's balls."

KEVIN MAURER is an award-winning journalist and best-selling co-author of *No Easy Day*, a first-hand account of the raid to kill Osama bin Laden. Before moving to Wilmington, Maurer covered the military at the *Fayetteville Observer*. A graduate of Old Dominion University in Norfolk, Virginia, he has lived and worked in North Carolina since 2003.

Views from Before

Esther, Andy & Me
(The Whole Bloomin' Weekend)

Azalea Festival 1958

NAN GRAHAM

NOWADAYS, the reigning queen of the North Carolina Azalea Festival is likely to be the star of a daytime or nighttime soap opera. The Queen's Court is made up of local beauty queens.

But in April 1958, Wilmington's annual spring Azalea Festival was somewhat different. The queen was a film actress and the beauty court was made up of North Carolina May Queens. It was the festival's eleventh year, and Azalea Queen XI was glamorous movie star Esther Williams. The wholesomely beautiful swimmer–movie star–athlete was at the top of her game with a string of Technicolor extravaganzas under her latex—a box-office sensation from 1949–1956.

What an image: that Amazonian height, those dazzling teeth, the perfect flower-entwined braided hair, which, according to *Photoplay* magazine, was immobilized with a mixture of baby oil and Vaseline. And those breathtaking dives from forty-foot towers into lighted circles of orchids and swimmers, choreographed by the legendary Busby Berkeley. You only need to have seen one of the dozen or so waterlogged flicks starring Williams to retrieve images of this stunning woman. (*Neptune's Daughter* and *Jupiter's Darling* are personal favorites.) Most teenage girls growing up at the time practiced her famous backstroke and dazzling Ipana smile each summer at local swimming pools.

In the Fifties, Queen Azalea's court included fourteen May Queens from college campuses all over North Carolina: Duke, Salem, Meredith, Wake Forest, Queens, St. Mary's. *Everybody* had a May Queen . . . except one university.

The University of North Carolina at Chapel Hill had no such queen. But they did have a "Beat Dook" Queen, chosen to reign over the uber-competitive Carolina-Duke parade and football game every fall. Yes, there was such a title. And it was mine. So I was delegated as the default UNC representative and sent to hobnob with celebrities on my first visit to Wilmington.

Each girl in the court was assigned a specific azalea color for her strapless net gown and matching parasol. The material for the dresses was ordered from New York City and custom dyed to match the flower. Actual azaleas were packed in Spanish moss and shipped to Manhattan for an exact azalea color match. The results were striking. Billowing net dresses (complete with crinoline underskirts) of pale pink, vermillion, rose, lavender, and purple were a knockout when the court clustered around Esther at the lawn parties for "photo ops." Of course, that phrase did not exist in 1958. Rolling down Third Street through downtown Wilmington on the court's float, we were a mass of human azaleas.

It's a good thing the human azaleas were there; the real azaleas were conspicuously absent. A cold snap had cancelled their appearance at their own festival. Carolina Finley, May Queen from Greensboro College, recalls that scores of potted hot-house azaleas were lugged in at every event as stand-ins for the real McCoy.

My designated azalea color was *Formosa,* that deep fuchsia hue so prevalent in the Low Country gardens. My dress and parasol were a perfect match to the real flower, but the color proved difficult to wear. The formosa-colored outfit turned my complexion a sallow, jaundiced

142

shade, providing a startling color contrast. I was a bit peeved that Duke's May Queen, Elizabeth Hanford (later to be nationally known as Elizabeth "Liddy" Dole), was assigned the more flattering rosy hue of the *Pride of Mobile* azalea. I secretly wondered if some malevolent Duke festival official had had a hand in assigning the color choices.

Other celebrity guests included the hunky John Bromfield (known mainly from the western TV series *Sheriff of Cochise*) and tough guy Scott Brady. Brady played the villain in numerous movies; he even had a fistfight scene with Clint Eastwood in the 1958 film *Ambush at Cimarron Pass*—the first and last time Eastwood was ever bested! (Eastwood famously said, "It was probably the worst western ever made.") Turns out that Brady was a real-life scoundrel, despite his ironic billing as the "King of Hospitality" in the Azalea Festival souvenir programs and all publicity. When his feud (causes unknown) with Queen Esther exploded, the King of Hospitality hastily departed Wilmington in a huff . . . mid-festival. *Note:* Mr. Brady was the last ever King of Hospitality. The position was eliminated the very next year.

One young actor, Andy Griffith, had recently made quite a name for himself with his hit recording of his comedy monologue, "What It Was, Was Football," a country preacher's wacky tale of attending his first football game. He was the latest sensation in the comedy field, selling over one million records the first year of the release, which garnered him a spot on *The Ed Sullivan Show*.

Griffith got on the elevator in the lobby at the Cape Fear Hotel that first day of the festival with a gaggle of the girls in the Queen's Court. "Anybody here representing Chapel Hill?" he asked.

I introduced myself to the engaging Mr. Griffith, proud that we shared the same alma mater. We chatted while the elevator rose to the fourth floor. The other May Queens were pea-green with envy that one of the celebrities had exchanged more than the usual superficial greeting—a real conversation—with the girl in unfortunate *Formosa*. During the festival, Andy always waved heartily every time he saw me, grinning that big Griffith smile and calling out, "Hey, Carolina!"

Our schedule was frantic but fun. Friday morning was the bridge dedication at Greenfield Lake Park, where city dignitaries and alligators gathered to extol the beauty of the water, the cypress trees, the naked azalea bushes, and the newly constructed footbridge. At 11 a.m., it was on to the Cottage Lane Outdoor Art Show where local artists exhibited their work along the narrow alleyway in the shadow of the First Presbyterian Church. Next, the Airlie Gardens luncheon, where we were welcomed by our hosts, the Corbetts, under the three-hundred-year-old Airlie live oak, a showstopper in their garden. Then a late afternoon cocktail party at Fergus' Ark, where we were allowed to wear street clothes and looked more like the hip college girls we were rather than escapees from Tara. Finally, we ended our day with a dance at the Cape Fear Country Club. Not a schedule for the weak of knee.

Fergus' Ark, no longer a working boat, floated at the foot of Market Street in the Cape Fear River, permanently secured to the dock. I remember it vividly, not only because of the unique setting, but because it was my first encounter with smoked oysters on toast points. I promptly decided that the delicacy was the ultimate hors d'oeuvre. Up until then, my Alabama self considered celery stuffed with pimiento cheese haute cuisine.

The grand Azalea Festival parade down Third Street kicked off Saturday's activities. We waved vigorously not only in our effort to appear royal, but to stave off hypothermia in the chilly morning air. Then on to a luncheon at the Surf Club before the Kings' Coronation at Brogden Hall. The final event was the big Coronation Ball at Lumina Pavilion, a turn-of-the-century beachfront building overlooking the Atlantic Ocean at Wrightsville Beach. The architectural beauty was beginning to look a bit like Miss Havisham's wedding cake, but you could still see how magnificent it must have been in its heyday. The spacious dance floor at Lumina was spectacular with enormous revolving mirrored balls, their glittering facets splattering lights across the polished oak floor.

I even had an up-close-and-personal encounter at Lumina with the Million Dollar Mermaid herself. In the ladies' room, Esther Williams was peering into the large mirror over the vanity. She was as beautiful up close as she was from afar. She pressed that perfect hair into place and took a sip from her drink on the vanity in front of her. I wondered if she used Vaseline on tonight's hairdo. This night her hair was pinned up with fresh white orchids woven into the braids, topped by the queen's tiara. Since we were the only two in the powder room and her back was to me, I had the perfect opportunity to stare.

Esther's shoulders were incredibly wide, the shoulders of a linebacker . . . or a professional swimmer. Turns out, she was in the midst of a meltdown from a wardrobe malfunction. Her heavy strapless satin dress had come unhooked in the back, and she made no bones about expressing her frustration and discomfort. Her royal dress was impossible to maneuver. She asked if I could help her out.

As I struggled with the annoyed queen's uncooperative hooks, I was engulfed in a stream of curses. The mushroom of air was blue with her salty language, generously laced with F-bombs. Remember, this was the South in 1958. I had only read these words in books. After all, I was a Tuscaloosa girl; only Birmingham girls used that kind of language. Thankfully the cuss words were not aimed at me, but at her unruly dress. I finally closed the last pesky hook and breathed a sigh of relief. Queen Azalea XI took a long, slow, regal swig from her drink. I had already heard her *usual* was vodka on the rocks. How decadent! How glamorous! How grand! And I was a tiny sequin in this glittery, glitzy Hollywood world.

I saw Andy Griffith in a Wilmington restaurant decades later, before he retired from the locally filmed *Matlock*. My lunch buddies spotted him and pointed him out. I had not seen him in person in five decades. Andy glanced briefly at us as we passed his table leaving the restaurant. Our eyes met for a second. Then he looked away. He didn't say, "Hey, Carolina!"

NAN GRAHAM is the author of *In a Magnolia Minute* and *Turn South at the Next Magnolia*. A graduate of the University of North Carolina at Chapel Hill, she received her graduate degree from The Citadel in Charleston. She has taught first grade, high school, and college, and is a long-time commentator for public radio station WHQR. Her on-air byline, "a lifelong Southerner," reveals the focus of her humorous commentaries on growing up and growing old in the South.

Fort Fisher, 150 Years Later

WILEY CASH

WE ARE SINGING HAPPY BIRTHDAY to my nephew over the sound of cannon fire. The Confederate Army has set up a position on the beach just north of the aquarium where we're eating cake and Domino's pizza on a Sunday afternoon in mid-January. It's my nephew's first birthday, and it's also the one hundred and fiftieth anniversary of the battle of Fort Fisher. At the exact moment my nephew buries both his hands in birthday cake, Union troops stream over the ramparts of the fort's earthen bulwarks. Re-enactments have been going on all weekend in honor of the anniversary, and while I watch my nephew open presents with his parents' help, I can't help but mark the strangeness of men pretending to kill one another while we're enjoying an everyday right-of-passage less than a mile away.

Fort Fisher sits on a narrow strip of land at the mouth of the Cape Fear River. Although it's only twenty miles south of Wilmington, it seems much farther. In the waning days of the Civil War, Fort Fisher ensured Wilmington's role as the Confederacy's last major port in the face of Union blockades of weapons and supplies. The fort's fall on January 15, 1865, was the death knell of the Confederacy. Three months later, Lee would surrender to Grant at Appomattox, an event that is just as well known as the first shots fired at Fort Sumter and the battles at Antietam, Manassas, Gettysburg, Chickamauga, and Shiloh. Unlike those events, the battle of Fort Fisher lives in relative obscurity despite its central role in the war. This is especially ironic in that North Carolina contributed more troops to the Confederacy than any other state, and it suffered the highest loss of life in the CSA as well.

When the birthday party ends, my wife and four-month-old daughter stay behind to tour the aquarium, and I set off on foot in the direction of the cannon fire with the hope of learning why I and many other Southerners know so little about Fort Fisher.

Approaching the fort in 2015, I imagine approaching it in 1865: As my eye travels east to west, the wind-swept dunes give way to groundsel, wax myrtles, yaupon trees, and live oaks so twisted and battered by centuries of weather they appear frozen in a constant state of being toppled. On the fort's southern edge, I stumble upon an empty Confederate camp beneath a stand of oak trees, the white canvas tents still wet from the previous night's heavy rain, campfires smoldering in the damp air. On the other side of the camp at the base of the fort's remaining earthen works, a group of a few hundred onlookers watch as dozens of Union and Confederate regiments kneel before a podium where a lecturer holds forth on the reconciliation between North and South that began with the fall of Fort Fisher.

When the talk is over and the troops disperse—some at the command of their officers, others alone or in small groups—I approach a tall, bearded Confederate, his face smudged with dirt and his rifle slung over his shoulder. His name is Christopher Graham, and he's a visiting professor of history at the University of North Carolina at Greensboro. I ask him why Fort Fisher is largely absent from Civil War lore. He stares before him and thinks about my question for a moment. "All hope for the success of the Confederacy is in Lee's army, and it dies at Appomattox." He smiles and nods at the passing soldiers—Confederate and Union—who are leaving the assembly. "The Confederacy dying all around Lee didn't get much attention, especially in North Carolina."

Dennis Brooks of Siler City, North Carolina, who with his white beard and stately manner could've easily been mistaken for Robert E. Lee if not for his Union blues, shares a similar sentiment. "Lee's surrender at Appomattox is what everybody knows about," he says. "Read the newspapers that were printed at that time, and read how little there is about North Carolinians."

All told, over 2,000 men died during the siege on Fort Fisher, and while I walk around the site's grounds, poking my head in and out of tents where Civil War memorabilia is being sold and nineteenth-century daguerreotypes are being made of kids in sneakers and sweatshirts, I can't help but feel strange about commemorating something so horrible as war by choosing to re-create it, and I also struggle with what seems to be popular opinion among the re-enactors: Fort Fisher's role in the war has been overlooked in favor of larger battles and grander moments.

A few hours later, my wife calls and says she and our daughter are leaving the aquarium and will stop by and pick me up at the entrance to the fort. On my way out to the road, I find myself in step with a father and son in period dress. The man wears the gray jacket and pants of a Confederate infantryman, and so does his son, who can't be any older than twelve. As we cross the road and head for the parking area along the beach, the father and son turn and look back at the fort. The crowds have thinned and there are more civilians wandering around with rebel flags and Pepsi cans than there are re-enactors wearing muddy boots with rifles in hand. The campfires have been extinguished, and men who'd already dressed for their rides home are taking down their tents. Although the sun is out and the day has warmed, the late afternoon scene feels somber.

The man and his son stand there for a moment longer, and then I watch them turn and walk toward the parking lot. It is January 18, 2015, and the one hundred and fiftieth anniversary of the battle for Fort Fisher is coming to an end; on this same day in 1865, the Civil War was effectively coming to an end as well. Perhaps that's why the role of Fort Fisher has been obscured by history: In the nostalgic South we don't always celebrate endings because they're so often accompanied by the difficult business of letting go.

WILEY CASH is the *New York Times* best-selling author of *A Land More Kind Than Home* and *This Dark Road to Mercy*. He teaches in the low-residency MFA program in fiction and nonfiction writing at Southern New Hampshire University. A native of North Carolina, he lives in Wilmington with his wife and daughter.

Color Meets Light

SUSAN TAYLOR BLOCK

THE HISTORY OF Wilmington's St. James Episcopal Church is a story of the city itself. In my mind, the narrative appears like a series of stained glass windows that radiate color when activated by light. Jewel-like, the windows tell true tales of an unlikely nature. Both the city and the church share a history that is quirky and filled with twists and turns. Both, too, have been the point of contact with an unusual number of famed people "from away."

In Colonial days, the Cape Fear River was similar to a leg of today's interstate highway system. At that time, the river led people of diverse backgrounds into a land ripe with opportunity. The busy waterway brought all sorts, ranging from the prosperous seeking more prosperity to those simply looking to escape. The river's stained glass window I see depicts a Cape Fear sunset in all its reflected glory of peach and azure laced with streaks of fiery orange.

St. James Parish had bureaucratic beginnings. It was the church of state, and services were held in the yellow courthouse building that sat in the middle of the intersection of Front and Market streets — just a block from the river. It was a two-story building with a hint of a steeple. Most likely, that is where the first vestry of St. James Anglican Church met in 1729.

The charter vestry was made up almost entirely of wealthy planters, most of whom they believed had, through blood or marriage, a tie to elegant, fiery Rory O'More, one of the principle organizers of the Irish Rebellion of 1641. The O'Mores (later changed to Moores) had been Roman Catholics for centuries, but many became Anglicans after Oliver Cromwell defeated them during the 1649 massacre at Drogheda. Rory O'More's descendants — King Roger, Maurice, and Nathaniel Moore — owned plantations on the west side of the Cape Fear: Orton, Kendal, and York. These planters were sons of Governor James Moore of South Carolina. I can see an image of a window of that bright yellow courthouse with its arched first floor entries — and folks in Colonial garb coming and going.

As Royalists, the vestry set about to erect a church that would bring both spiritual refreshment and patriotic zeal. Prior to moving to Cape Fear, the James Moores had ties to St. James Church in Goose Creek, near Charleston. Royalist touches adorned the Goose Creek church and, doubtless, did so in the first St. James building in Wilmington. Just as the vestry kept the king in mind, so did George II keep the Moores in mind during one transatlantic political battle. The king referred to them as "those pestiferous Moores" — an oblique compliment for sure.

St. James Churchyard reflects the melting pot nature of Wilmington's early years. The individuals interned in its burying ground ran the gamut from the rather famous, like arch-Patriot Cornelius Harnett, to unfortunate sailors who happened to drown in the Cape Fear River or die of disease while in port. They came from all over — Baltimore, Philadelphia, Boston, New York, Bermuda, Nova Scotia, Ireland, Scotland, England, and France. But now their remains abide together in one of Wilmington's most naturally preserved Colonial spaces.

The churchyard, a study of grays, would not translate well into stained glass, but local color certainly showed itself there on October 31, 1765. By that time, the Moore family's Royalist leanings slanted in a different direction. Superior Court Justice Maurice Moore Jr. had recently penned a pamphlet protesting England's taxation of the colonies.

151

Judge Moore followed up his writings with action as he, with family and friends, began to participate in impassioned and creative demonstrations of their feelings. So, on All Hallow's Eve, 1765, Patriots staged a mock funeral lit only by the dancing light of a bonfire. The corpse of "Liberty" was found to have a weak pulse just before *his* coffin was lowered into a freshly dug grave. Jubilant Patriots removed the "Liberty" effigy from the coffin, placed him in a large chair with arms, then gathered round to voice their feelings to him.

That colorfully dressed Tory, Banastre Tarleton, would make a grand stained glass window subject, except that he was the enemy. For eighteen days during the American Revolution, British General Charles Cornwallis commandeered the Burgwin-Wright House located across the street from St. James Church. Lieutenant Colonel Banastre Tarleton, depicted in his portrait as something of a clothes horse, was in Wilmington, too. Tales abound, but it does seem that they misused the church to some degree. According to legend, Tarleton sheltered his real horses inside St. James Church. The story echoed during the Civil War when Yankees occupied Wilmington and damaged the church.

The issue of race relations in Wilmington reached its nadir with the infamous Riot of 1898, but it was a St. James rector, Dr. Adam Empie, who, beginning in 1811, spoke most fervently against racism. A special breed of clergymen, Empie exercised his robust intellectual powers, yet was passionate in living and expressing his faith. He approached the subject of slavery by crediting the Bible as his authority; he used his mastery of Hebrew and Greek—languages far richer in vocabulary than English—to understand the words in their original languages. His diligent studies led him to become an outspoken and unflinching Abolitionist who encouraged the building of galleries in the St. James sanctuary so that enslaved people could worship there too.

Empie, a native of Schenectady, New York, married a Southerner named Ann Eliza Wright in 1814. Ironically, her dowry included several slaves. Empie tried to free them, but they refused to leave, protesting that his benevolence toward them meant more. It is rumored that at least one of the Empies' slaves was buried in their family plot at Oakdale Cemetery, but this has not been proved.

Adam Empie represents well the Wilmington phenomena of distinguished leaders from afar who inspire and improve. After serving until 1814 at St. James, he and Ann Eliza moved to West Point where he assumed his new job as the chaplain of the U.S. Military Academy. In 1827, he began nine years of service as president of the College of William and Mary in Williamsburg, where he also served as rector of Bruton Parish Church. When he sought to include slaves at services there, protests were so pronounced that he began looking for another post. Empie's last parish was in Richmond where in 1837 he helped organize St. James Episcopal Church, named after his beloved post in Wilmington. He encouraged the creation of slave galleries in the existing white churches in Richmond, and founded a slave mission on Broad Street where he taught Bible lessons. His work during this period was rewarded posthumously when he was named "A Maker of Richmond" in the 1940s.

When I think of Dr. Empie, I imagine a stained glass window in which he is depicted high up in the elevated pulpit of the Colonial church. In the pews sit the many African American workmen, artists, carpenters, and other artisans who helped build St. James's church buildings and whose names are unknown to us. The dominant color would be royal blue: royal to honor the nobility of hard work and the use of God-given talents — and blue to depict the sadness of it all.

The warmth of the color red permeates the window I see for 1839, when St. James dedicated a brand new building. Architect Thomas U. Walter, famous for designing the U.S. Capitol dome, designed the Gothic Revival St. James that still stands. Other famed architects were responsible for buildings that now are part of the St. James campus. Architect Hobart Upjohn designed the 1923 parish house, and Henry Bacon, architect of the Lincoln Memorial, designed the Ann Moore Bacon Church House for his friend, Donald MacRae in 1902. Henry Bacon lived in Wilmington during his youth and became close friends with siblings Hugh MacRae, Donald MacRae, and Agnes MacRae Parsley. Though Bacon generally shirked residential design, he drew magnificent house plans for all three MacRaes because of his love for the family. Although there is a distant genealogical connection, the Ann Moore Bacon House is not renamed for any of Henry Bacon's close kin, but the late Ann Bacon did happen to be a direct descendant of charter vestryman King Roger Moore.

The church continues to echo the history of Wilmington itself in its ability to attract attention. The materialized dreams of other famous architects still exist in the port city, but perhaps the ultimate example of attention of any sort occurred when movie director Dino De Laurentiis discovered Wilmington in 1986. Now maybe the world, but certainly the nation, has discovered our city, too. Movies and television series have placed the city on the vacation-stop map. Guides give tours to relate what scene was shot where. And the scruffy stranger seated at the next table just might be someone most teenagers would recognize. The various scenes that have been shot at St. James help pay the repair bills for a building now quite aged. Such a source of revenue would be a big surprise for Thomas U. Walter.

Quirks abound. St. James is a municipal landmark to many and a beloved worship aid to some. It is a building that houses a seventeenth-century painting of Jesus, once stolen by Spanish pirates, then salvaged by a group of Brunswick County residents—one of whom was a liquor vendor named *Dry*. The painting was then given to the church by the state of North Carolina, in place of funds the church requested from the state. St. James sits above an eighteenth-century underground tunnel that was created to drain the puddled city, but is also rumored to have been used as an escape route for slaves.

The first St. James building, later replaced, jutted out into Market Street. Some churchgoers were buried there. A few of the bodies were moved before the current Market Street was excavated and paved, but the bones of others, like illustrious businessman John Ancrum, remain.

At the busy intersection of Third and Market streets, St. James sits with its Gothic arches pointing upward and its parapet, which like the Gothic arch, draws one's eyes toward heaven. New members are added steadily, yet a few descendants of the 1729 vestry remain. . . . I see a stained glass window. A brilliant rainbow arcs above two blocks—from the tower of St. James Episcopal Church to the roof of City Hall.

Wilmington native **SUSAN TAYLOR BLOCK** works as a historian who researches and writes about southeastern North Carolina. Her writings range from photo anthologies to detailed histories, such as *Temple of Our Fathers: St. James Episcopal Church (1729–2004)*. In her less serious moments, she enjoys writing light verse, some of which can be found online at susantaylorblock.com.

Views from 1898 & Beyond

A Tale of Two Cities

PHILIP GERARD

FOR A BRIEF TIME I ENJOYED the extraordinary experience of living in two Wilmingtons at the same time — one hundred years apart.

The occasion was the centennial commemoration of what was probably the most shameful episode in our city's history, the white supremacist coup of 1898. I had written about it several years prior in a novel called *Cape Fear Rising* and found myself ambushed by the storm of controversy the book aroused.

While researching the book I had walked the ground, retracing the steps of the perpetrators and victims along Market Street and Seventh, down along the riverfront, deep into the garden of stone monuments at the Oakdale Cemetery, and out to the cold, drizzly November reaches of Smith Creek.

During that period of about a year, I dreamed a recurring dream.

It is night, the familiar downtown along the river cast in the dubious glow of gas lamps. I am walking a deserted street when I notice a dim, yellowish light emanating from a corner store. The door is slightly ajar, and I enter.

No one is there. But another door leading to a backroom is also ajar, and through it leaks a pool of light. I slowly open that door and enter the room. Men dressed in old-fashioned dark suits, high collars, and vests are seated at a long wooden table, smoking cigars and speaking in low, conspiratorial tones. They don't notice me. In fact, I seem invisible. They carry on.

What they are doing is plotting the overthrow of the government of Wilmington.

I listen, and from their nightly secret meetings, I learn the story.

In its outlines, the story is simple. On November 10, 1898, a cadre of local businessmen and politicians, acting in concert with the North Carolina "Redeemer" Democratic Party, steamrolled its way to a victory in the state-wide and federal elections. In addition to the usual tricks like stuffing ballot boxes, the Redeemers used armed "Red Shirts" to keep blacks from voting.

At the time, the population of Wilmington was about 25,000 — 17,000 blacks and 8,000 whites. The Redeemer movement was designed to put blacks in their place and put the white oligarchy back in charge. Its architect was Furnifold Simmons, head of the state Democratic Party.

The firebrand who led the local effort was an ex-Confederate colonel from Hillsborough named Alfred Moore Waddell. On the eve of the election, he delivered a sizzling speech from the stage of Thalian Hall in which he admonished his audience, "If you see the Negro out voting, tell him to go home. If he refuses, kill him! Shoot him down in his tracks!"

Furthermore, he promised his audience of so-called Anglo-Saxons, "We will prevail if we have to choke the Cape Fear River with the carcasses of our enemies!"

Not satisfied with taking over the legislature and governor's mansion, as well as just electing John D. Bellamy, another prominent white supremacist, to Congress, the Redeemer Democrats wanted to replace Wilmington's Republican mayor and city aldermen (white and black)— legally elected in 1896 and not subject to reelection in 1898—with their own men. In effect, they intended to put an end once and for all to the policies of Reconstruction.

They drafted a White Declaration of Independence, signed by more than four hundred leading citizens, and issued an ultimatum to a committee drafted from the black community. The pretext for that ultimatum was an editorial written by Alex Manly, editor of the *Daily Record*, Wilmington's African American newspaper.

Manly's editorial was essentially a rebuttal to the speech delivered on the subject of lynching by Rebecca Latimer Felton, wife of a Georgia congressman who herself would go on to serve as a U.S. senator. She claimed that the biggest danger to white farmwives in the South was being raped by "black brutes."

She exhorted her audience,

> When there is not enough religion in the pulpit to organize a crusade against sin; nor justice in the court house to promptly punish crime; nor manhood enough in the nation to put a sheltering arm about innocence and virtue — if it needs lynching to protect woman's dearest possession from the ravening human beasts — then I say lynch, a thousand times a week if necessary.

The *Daily Record* editorial claimed that sometimes white women were attracted to black men. "Don't ever believe that your women can remain pure while you are debauching ours," it warned. "You sow the seed, the harvest will come in time."

The editorial was published on August 18, 1898, a full year after Felton's speech, and went largely unnoticed — until it was picked up by the white newspaper, the *Messenger*, which ran it on the front page every day from August 24 until election day next to a new report of an alleged black atrocity.

The white supremacists demanded that *Daily Record* editor Manly "leave town forever" within twenty-four hours, and that Manly's answer to their ultimatum be received by early the next morning. For reasons known only to himself, the man entrusted with Manly's conciliatory reply did not deliver it by hand by the deadline, but instead mailed it.

With no response from the Committee of Colored Citizens, Alfred Moore Waddell led an armed mob of white men and boys from the Wilmington Light Infantry (WLI) Armory on Market Street to the offices of the *Daily Record*. A local militia company, the WLI had missed the Spanish-American War in Cuba, including the charge up San Juan Hill. They were spoiling for a fight. The mob shot a young black man who opened the door to the newspaper offices and then burned the place to the ground, even holding off the black fire brigade at gunpoint so they could not douse the fire.

Returning home, the Waddell mob encountered a crowd of blacks a few blocks away, who had gathered to find out what all the commotion was. The white mob started shooting, and the violence continued for three days.

Between November 10 and November 13, 1898, people were killed. There has never been an accurate count of the dead. No official figure was ever published—because there was no investigation. Estimates range from a low of a dozen or so to hundreds. The victims mostly died by gunfire in the streets, some in front of firing squads. Many others were beaten, arrested, driven from town.

All the dead were black.

By some accounts, at the height of the violence, wagonloads of bodies were dumped into the river, though many historians dismiss such reports as mere legend, inspired (they surmise) by Waddell's fiery speech.

Democratic white supremacists took power of the city at gunpoint and banished the former aldermen and mayor. A list was drawn up of "undesirables": A few whites, such as Benjamin F. Keith—a ship's chandler and warehouse owner—and nearly every prominent black politician, businessman, and professional man in town were on it. They were rounded up at bayonet point and forced onto trains destined for points out of town.

"The Light Infantry squad has much to answer for," wrote one contemporary eyewitness about that organization's killing spree in the black community. "They shot down right and left in a most unlawful way, killing one man who was simply standing at a corner waiting to get back to his work."

Eyewitnesses reported that the WLI conducted firing squads.

George Rountree, the lawyer and later judge who acted as a kind of house counsel to the secret groups who planned the coup, was elected to the statehouse as a direct result of his work on the white supremacists' behalf. Once in Raleigh, he helped to craft an ingenious piece of legislation, usually referred to as the grandfather clause (also known as the disenfranchisement clause) as part of a state constitutional amendment.

James L. Hunt, historian of law at Mercer University, describes the grandfather clause this way:

> [It] was an important component of the 1900 constitutional amendment restricting North Carolina's class of eligible voters. The disfranchisement amendment provided that voters must be able to read and write a section of the state constitution in the English language and to pay a poll tax. Far from attempting to encourage literacy, however, the primary goal of the amendment, as admitted in the Democratic Party's pro-amendment campaign in 1900, was to eliminate African American voters as a factor in North Carolina politics.

So the event was a big deal, and its effect was to stifle black voting rights until 1964.

When the centennial commemoration rolled around in 1998, I was squarely in the middle of research. I proposed to the local public radio affiliate that we stage a radio drama of the events, and Aileen LeBlanc, a daring producer, made it happen. It was entitled *1898: An American Coup.*

My idea was to use a *War of the Worlds* scenario. We would begin with a local news broadcast—with a twist: The "news" would be the election results of 1898. Then routine classical programming would come on for a few minutes until interrupted by Aileen LeBlanc as news director reporting that a mob was marching on Free Love Hall, home of the *Daily Record.*

She would dispatch correspondents to report firsthand from the field. We would all live the story in real time, with the same confusion, conflicting eyewitness accounts, and incomplete facts as if we were covering a contemporary breaking news story.

The conceit was simple: Inside the radio station, it was, technologically, 1998 — so we could record, play archival tape, broadcast telephone interviews, and so on. But outside on the streets of Wilmington, it was 1898 — with streetcars, horse-drawn fire engines, cotton compresses, and so on.

We had a tight production schedule, which meant that we were immersed in the events of 1898 Wilmington — not a pleasant place to be, you might imagine — in a windowless studio for long trackless hours, coaching and directing actors, recording scenes, then sitting at the Roland digital board, editing and adding sound effects.

But here's the thing: Making the radio drama was an uplifting, even inspiring experience.

Looking back, it seems to me the joy came in three parts — over and above the satisfaction of telling the true story on the air and achieving some measure of rectitude all those generations later.

Part one was working with Aileen. She had always been a fearless champion of the underdog, and she had reshaped the way the radio station addressed issues of public and social concern through brave reporting and fighting for coverage of the black community — and acting on her convictions put her job in jeopardy. Local public radio, dependent on donor support and business underwriting, can tend to shy away from controversy as fast as any commercial station. (Even a couple of national NPR personalities she enlisted to play themselves in the drama were, at the last minute, forced to withdraw from the project by their bosses in Washington.)

Aileen's technical skills matched her sterling ethics. What she was able to do with a handful of actors — none of whom were paid — in a few days in the studio was sheer magic.

The second part of the joy lay in working with the cadre of actors she assembled — including Madafo Lloyd Wilson, who produces the nationally syndicated winter holiday program *A Season's Griot*; Ed Kearney, a TV and movie actor who delivered Waddell's stirring and horrifying speeches; Tony Rivenbark, long the reigning genius of Thalian Hall, who took his star-turn as Furnifold Simmons, the head of the state Redeemer Democrats; and others, including Steve Taylor, Jerry Adams, Eric Paisley, Perry Fisher, and Shawn Mitchell.

The radio and TV reporters were amazing to work with: Rhonda Bellamy, Harvard Jennings, Scott Simpson, Jon Evans, Pat Marriott, Jemila Erickson, and George Scheibner. All of them showed an enthusiasm for the project and great range. It's hard to play yourself as a fictional reporter in another age, but they were all so convincing that I still get choked up listening to them.

Everyone played multiple roles. The African American actors in particular got a kick out of playing both their black counterparts in 1898 and members of the white supremacist mob, shouting racial epithets at each other and then answering back—for once in control of the story.

For all of us, *1898: An American Coup* turned out to be an emotional experience, grabbing us in unexpected ways. You can hear it in the voices of the actors, working from my script but also extemporizing at key moments, their steady professional cadence going all a-stutter, their calm tone faltering with real horror and empathy.

The third part of my satisfaction came from the fieldwork we pursued in gathering authentic sound. To record Kearney as Colonel Waddell working the crowd at Thalian Hall into a manic froth, Aileen recorded him in the studio and added reverb to give his voice live presence. But we didn't want to use canned applause—that would be too tame. So we got permission from Thalian Hall to address the audience at the premiere of *Big River* before the play.

At the appointed moment, we walked onstage, Aileen carrying the portable recording gear. I looked out and saw the same kind of capacity crowd Waddell had seen that fateful night, filling the same vintage theater from mezzanine to balcony. I said, "Okay, when I give the signal, give me some weak applause and hold it till I signal stop." I gave the signal, and, remarkably, they did.

Next I said, "Okay, a little louder, just the men." And so they did. At last I called on everyone to applaud ecstatically, to pound their chairs and cheer and hoot rebel yells, and so they did. And that all made it into the show, authentic sound from the site of that pivotal long-ago speech.

Members of the *Big River* cast later thanked Aileen. They said that they'd gotten the biggest ovation ever at their curtain call—and maybe we could stop by to prime the audience before every performance.

I also called on a former student of mine who was a deputy in the sheriff's department, and he arranged for a team of officers to meet me at the gunnery range and let me record live fire: shotguns, volley fire, single pistol shots, thirty-ought-sixes. So the gunfire in *1898: An American Coup* came from real guns fired outdoors—the same calibers of firearms used a hundred years before.

The final satisfaction came in the very act of editing. Aileen actually did all the editing digitally, but I sat with her as we worked out how to mix sounds and voices, including my own as a commentator. And also the rumble of Atlantic Coast Line trains, dogs barking, shrilling steam whistles on the river, horses' hooves pounding on cobblestones, and so on. It was thrilling to create a landscape of sound, one that conjured that cityscape of a hundred years ago.

The show came together just as we had hoped: The election news roundup for Thursday, November 10, 1898, followed by the Brandenburg Concerto #2 in F, then Aileen's interruption with breaking news. Cut to Scott Simpson reporting breathlessly from the mob at Free Love Hall, describing with shocked disbelief how the clapboard building has turned into an inferno. Then to me in the studio offering background to the events as a commentator.

We hear Manly's inflammatory editorial read by a member of the Black Ministerial Union. Back to Scott at the Alexander Sprunt Champion Compress down on the river, where a white vigilante committee is threatening workers with a Gatling gun. More cuts to Rhonda Bellamy in the middle of mob violence at Fourth and Harnett streets, retreating into a neighborhood store as gunshots shatter the windows. We revisit Colonel Waddell delivering the White Declaration of Independence from the taped archive, then turn to Scott at City Hall, as the mayor and board of alderman are forced to resign at gunpoint and Colonel Waddell is sworn in as mayor.

Midway through the broadcast, the story goes national, with Public Radio of America (PRA) picking up the thread and Jim Polson, in real life a reporter for Monitor Radio, bringing us up to date on events. The correspondents interview blacks on the streets, a white woman fleeing town on a train, Red Shirts gloating over the "blackbirds" they have shot, and a WLI sergeant banishing citizens onto trains at bayonet point.

The broadcast finishes with me reporting from Oakdale Cemetery, where hundreds of black families are hiding out under the dogwoods and wax myrtles to escape the vigilantes, with a cold rain soaking them as they murmur and sing. And I swear, when I recorded that segment I was right there, in that dark, rainy place, among the tombstones and those long-suffering people.

Today, whenever I listen to it, I close my eyes and a hundred-odd years drop away. I am there again, crouched in the foggy midnight of that sanctuary of the dead, lost in time, saying once more, "They don't know what new terrors tomorrow will bring. They're just trying to make it through this long night. The Devil is loose in Wilmington tonight. The city is in chaos. The social contract has broken down. Good people have done terrible things to their own neighbors. Other good people failed to stop them. When the sun comes up, we'll find out what is left of our beautiful city. It will take the best that is in all of us to put the pieces of our civic life back together again. Let us hope we rise to the occasion."

And even now, whenever I walk the streets of downtown, I still hear those ghosts murmuring to me, still hear the echo of that long-ago gunfire and the catcalls of the vigilantes, still hear those black voices crying out in rage and pain and disbelief. Still listen to the low voices of those men in black suits gathered around that long table in that secret backroom meeting, plotting their coup in my dreams.

I walk on, with one foot in each city.

PHILIP GERARD is the author of nine books of fiction and nonfiction, most recently *Down the Wild Cape Fear* and *The Patron Saint of Dreams*, winner of the 2012 Gold Medal for Nonfiction from the Independent Publisher. With his wife, Jill Gerard, he co-edits *Chautauqua*, the literary journal of Chautauqua Institution in New York. He teaches in the creative writing department at UNC Wilmington. His novel *The Dark of the Island* is forthcoming.

A Successful Coup d'*What*?

BERTHA BOYKIN TODD

MY TWIN SISTER, MYRTLE, AND I attended a comprehensive high school in Sampson County, North Carolina, where our father was that school's first principal. In my history classes, the teacher sometimes talked about a *coup d'état*. The word was quite foreign to me because all *coup d'état* events seemed to occur in distant countries. As a teenager, I never imagined that I would visit any of these countries that were so far away. Nonetheless, this term, *coup d'état*, lay deep in the recesses of my memory.

After graduating from high school, I attended North Carolina College (now North Carolina Central University) in Durham. In my world history classes, *coup d'état* was once again mentioned by my instructors. Since I was familiar with the *word*, now I had to learn its *definition*. But again, I noticed that each time this word was used, it was in reference to events that always occurred in foreign countries. By this time, I was motivated to discover just what events and/or actions resulted in a *coup d'état*. I continued to believe that *coups d'état* still occurred elsewhere, not in the United States.

When I graduated in 1952, it was time for me to seek employment. So I headed to Wilmington, where I was hired by the New Hanover County Board of Education as a media specialist. Little did I realize that I would spend my entire thirty-nine–year career in the city of Wilmington.

During my career, I served as an assistant principal at John T. Hoggard High School and also attended graduate school at East Carolina University (ECU). Even though the term *coup d'état* was not mentioned in any of my classes at ECU, it remained in the recesses of my mind.

Earlier in my tenure with the board of education, I was employed at Williston Industrial High School (later Williston Senior High School). It didn't take long for me to become keenly aware that there was little or no social interaction between the various ethnic groups. Any interaction that occurred appeared to be limited and/or strained. Since I believe that there is only one race—the human race—I prefer not to use the word *race* when describing ethnic groups. The thing that puzzled me most was the manner in which people of color would take me aside and whisper about violence that occurred in Wilmington in November of 1898. I observed that there was no open conversation regarding that event. Blacks and whites, I discovered several years later, would talk among themselves about it, but not with each other. It was only after my retirement that I began to learn much more about Wilmington's past.

Most of the schools in New Hanover County were desegregated in the late 1960s. During that time, members of the Ku Klux Klan held regular meetings regarding the efforts of desegregation. While I was assistant principal at John T. Hoggard High School, I had a white, male co-worker who volunteered to attend Klan meetings to find out what was being said. He informed me that several Klan members repeatedly stated at one meeting, "The blacks do not want a repeat performance of 1898."

During those years of school desegregation, many black citizens, on the other hand, were not volunteering in the community or making any public efforts to support this transformational process. Since I was pretty active, I wondered about their reluctance to become involved. Some of my questions were answered years later when I became a co-chair for the 1898 Centennial Foundation (later the 1898 Foundation).

Established in 1995, the 1898 Centennial Foundation was organized with one black and one white citizen serving as co-chairs. Each subcommittee also consisted of one black and one white co-chair. The subcommittees were as follows: the Ministerial Roundtable, Partners for Economic Inclusion, Education (Study Circles), and Memorial Fundraiser.

In 1996, a member of the 1898 Centennial Foundation approached me to request that I serve as the black co-chair for the organization. I reluctantly agreed to serve as an interim co-chair until a permanent replacement was found. I was hesitant to take it on because it was a difficult time for me. I was grieving the loss of my sister and my spouse who passed six weeks apart. That autumn, I discovered that my interim co-chair position would become permanent. I had to become mentally and emotionally ready to undertake this position. I served as co-chair from 1996–99.

The 1898 Foundation's philosophy, which I wrote, was as follows:

> No one living in Wilmington today was a participant in the events of 1898. Consequently, none among us bears any personal responsibility for what happened. But all among us — no matter our race or history, whether we have arrived here only recently or come from families that have called Wilmington home for generations — are responsible for 1998. On each of us falls the personal responsibility to make our community one where economic justice and racial harmony flourish.
>
> *Surely this is a challenge we are willing to accept.*
>
> —Bertha Boykin Todd

The 1898 Foundation mission statement was as follows:

> to *tell the story* of 1898 and to make the real history known;
> to *heal the wounds* of the racial division which continue in the city;
> to *honor the memory* of those who lost lives and property in 1898; and
> to *restore the hope* through efforts to foster economic inclusion.

On November 10, 1998, the members of the 1898 Centennial Foundation sponsored a program at Thalian Hall to commemorate those individuals who were run out of town and those individuals who lost their lives on November 10, 1898.

The 1898 Foundation was dissolved in 2009, but during its thirteen years (1995–2008), a great deal of research was conducted to verify the events that occurred in the 1800s in the city of Wilmington. I finally began to get answers to old, unanswered questions about the reason for the strained relationships between blacks and whites. This exploration of history conducted by members of the foundation brought to light the fact that Wilmington is the only city in the United States to have experienced a successful *coup d'état*.

Consider the following:

Wilmington was the largest city in the state of North Carolina in the 1800s. In the 1890s, a new Populist Party (mostly white, wheat farmers) joined with Republicans (mostly blacks and some whites) to form a new party called the Fusionists, while each maintained its original party. The Fusionist alliance in 1894 swept the state, capturing control of the state legislature. It was particularly strong in Wilmington.

This Fusionist majority rewrote the state's restrictive election laws, significantly increasing black participation in state and local politics for the first time since Reconstruction.

As a result, Republican Daniel Russell of Wilmington was elected governor in 1896. The Fusionists retained control of the state legislature while winning control of a number of municipal governments including that of Wilmington. The Democrats, having lost control of state and municipal governments for the first time since Reconstruction began, resolved to regain power in 1898.

For several months before the '98 elections, the news media through-out the state began to spread messages regarding race and the Fusionists (Populists and Republicans), aimed at undermining the alliance. Additional voter-suppression strategies were used to reduce the number of members of the aforementioned two parties from voting in that year's November election.

A militia, referred to as the "Red Shirts," from Fayetteville came to Wilmington for several months to assist the Democratic Party with some of its voter-suppression tactics. Tensions ran high. Before and even after the election, the Red Shirts patrolled the city streets, intimidating blacks.

The voter-suppression strategies worked. The Democratic Party regained power. But violence erupted anyway, with Red Shirts and vigilante groups burning the city's black-owned newspaper. An unknown number of blacks were killed in the violence that followed. Many black and white members of the Fusionist Party were run out of town.

Even though installation of Wilmington's newly elected officials was scheduled to be held in January of 1899, these newly elected officials stormed city hall in November of 1898 and demanded that the current mayor, police chief, and members of the board of aldermen resign imme-diately. Alfred Waddell, a Democrat, became the new mayor leading a new all-white board of aldermen.

And so it was. The city of Wilmington, North Carolina, holds the dubious distinction of having been the location of the only successful *coup d'état* in the United States of America.

BERTHA BOYKIN TODD was a media specialist and administrator for the New Hanover County Public Schools for thirty-nine years. A graduate of North Carolina Central Univer-sity with advanced degrees from East Carolina University, she was awarded an honorary doctorate from the University of North Carolina at Wilmington. She is author and co-author of three books, including *My Restless Journey, Meet the Help: True Stories of Domestics,* and *The Visionary Five* (the history of Alpha Psi Omega Chapter of Alpha Kappa Alpha Sorority).

Our Past Is Current

JAMES LEUTZE

I HAD LIVED IN NORTH CAROLINA for twenty-five years before moving to Wilmington in 1990 to become chancellor at the University of North Carolina at Wilmington. My family had visited the city and I was well aware of its Civil War history. Although it seemed hard to believe as the twentieth century neared its end, up until the 1920 census, Wilmington had been the state's largest city. In 1990 it was a beautiful riverfront city that time had passed by—its glory days behind it. Gone from the downtown wharfs were most of the ocean-going ships. Gone was one of the South's biggest cotton exchanges. Gone were the busy docks on the shore across from the city where naval stores had been collected and shipped around the world. And gone was the Atlantic Coast Line Railroad that had once connected Wilmington to the rest of the country. Remaining was a somewhat dreamy, Spanish-moss–draped place—very proud of its past. It was a city where many were content to bask in past glories and let the rest of the world go by.

It didn't take long, however, for me to discover there were dark secrets haunting the streets of old Wilmington. The 1970s and 1980s had been decades of unrest in the South, and Wilmington had not been spared.

Integration and school desegregation, in particular, had rocked the region. Wilmington had its own violent confrontation that involved a group of protesters who became known as the *Wilmington Ten*. These ten men and women were jailed for participating in protests that had led to arson and the death of two people. Their trial got national headlines and was not the kind of publicity most cities want. Because of this and a national mood of uneasiness, I made it my business to cultivate contacts throughout Wilmington's diverse population. As chancellor of UNCW I knew that unrest in town could quickly spread to our campus, so I wanted to know people and have contacts with a variety of key community-based groups, including the black power structure.

My task was challenging—even harder than I'd anticipated. Wilmington's black community, like many socio-economic groups, wasn't monolithic. It was fragmented, depending on church membership, class, and place of work. Moreover, all of those groups had different leadership. More so, it was a challenge to reach consensus on just who the leadership was.

Finally, someone gave me an intriguing clue. "There is a leadership group," he said, "but we don't want you to know who they are . . ." "Why?" I asked. "Because, we know what you did last time." "Last time?" I asked. "1898" was the answer.

From this and other experiences I came to realize that nowhere had I found history so alive and relevant as in Wilmington.

What had happened in 1898? The answer split the community right down the middle. Many, maybe most, white citizens had no idea what 1898 conjured up. Most black people on the other hand even a century later had visceral memories or at least an oral tradition about what had gone on. But almost universally no one wanted to talk about it. You didn't have to dig too deeply to learn the outline of events.

In November 1898, there had been a race riot in Wilmington. Several participants had been killed; buildings had been burned; leading black citizens had been driven out of town and a new political leadership had been installed.

But beneath the broad outline, on which there was agreement, lay troublesome details and divergent stories. Part of the complexity resided in disagreement about what to call what happened. A *riot*, a *massacre*, or a *political coup?* Whereas the white community, if they knew about 1898, might differ on that last question, the black community did have a consensus — 1898 was a disgraceful event intended to intimidate them into passivity.

There were multiple factors that brought things to a head in 1898. There was, as always in the South, race. North Carolina struggled with adjusting to Reconstruction. The KKK and violent nightriders like the Red Shirts were relentless in intimidating black voters in the thirty years since the end of the war. They had been quite successful in rural North Carolina. In Wilmington, though, there were black police and firefighters. The highest-paid public official was the black federal customs collector. This, plus the fact that there was a black majority in town, fostered paranoia among some white citizens.

Lurking behind, or within this paranoia was the volatile issue of sex. Since at least the 1880s, rumors had swirled that black men were raping white women. And if they weren't raping them, they were making sexual advances. These highly charged suspicions naturally incited reactions from white men who, in that time, mythically viewed themselves as the protectors of fragile Southern women.

Enter Alexander Manly, a black man related to the white former North Carolina Governor Charles Manly and editor of the black newspaper, the *Daily Record*. Since the mid-1880s the issue of rape by black men had been a volatile one. Given his own background and sensing a good story, Manly published an editorial in the summer of 1898 saying that if white men took better care of their women maybe those women wouldn't be attracted to black men. If Manly had been trying to attract attention, he no doubt exceeded expectations. One of the rioters' first acts in November 1898 was to burn the *Daily Record* to the ground.

So race and sex were definitely factors. Maybe *the* primary factors. But there was a large element of politics as well. Since the Civil War, the

Democratic Party that from our contemporary vantage point can be called the anti-Lincoln Republican or Conservative Party had held power in North Carolina. To be sure, there was a Republican Party that got all the black votes and a not inconsiderable white vote. In part as a result of economic turmoil, in 1894 the Populists, many of whom were poor white farmers, joined with the Republicans and black voters in what was called a "fusionist" victory to throw the Democrats out.

From 1894 to 1898, the out-of-power Democrats waged an unprincipled, white-supremacist campaign. It was no holds barred, bare knuckled, led by the Raleigh *News & Observer,* as well as by future North Carolina luminaries, Furnifold Simmons and Charles B. Aycock. Because of its size and commercial importance, Wilmington was singled out by white supremacists as an example of corrupt Fusionist rule. Using the violence in the streets as cover that November, it was no surprise that Democrats marched into City Hall, threw out elected officials they disapproved of, and installed a new hand-picked leadership. All of this, of course, in the interest of "good government." Statewide, the Democrats re-won control and rewrote the state constitution to disenfranchise blacks. They also sent Furnifold Simmons to the U.S. Senate and Charles Aycock to the Governor's Mansion. For the next fifty years, these conservatives controlled North Carolina.

When I arrived, the state had taken a more progressive turn. Still our race problems weren't behind us, and hence my interest in learning about the city's leadership and its past. At least people were willing to talk. In 1994 Philip Gerard, a member of the UNCW English Department and a fellow contributor to *27 Views,* published a novel, *Cape Fear Rising—* a fictional account of the 1898 "insurrection" and its impact on the city, the state, and the South. In 1998 UNCW sponsored a series of lectures on the one hundredth anniversary of the events. The keynote was delivered by the late John Hope Franklin, the noted black historian. One positive outcome was the city established several committees to improve race relations. In addition, plans were made to erect a monument that would commemorate 1898 so that no one forgets.

Things aren't perfect in Wilmington. I am particularly concerned about what I see as current efforts to repress the black vote. But at least we are more open and honest about our past.

JAMES LEUTZE taught history for more than twenty years at the University of North Carolina at Chapel Hill before becoming president of Hampden-Sydney College in Virginia in 1987. He became chancellor of UNC Wilmington in 1990. He retired from that position in 2003. He has written two books that have won national prizes — one on American diplomatic history and the other a naval biography. His most recent book is titled *Welcome to North Carolina: Set Clocks Back 100 Years*. He and his wife live in Wilmington. He has five grandchildren.

The Evidence of Things Unforgotten
A Short Story

MARLON RACHQUEL MOORE

"IT SEEMS OUT OF PLACE AND ISOLATED."

"It sits on the edge of town and took me several U-turns to find it. When I finally did, I was surprised it was surrounded by dilapidated housing."

"I saw more signs for the police station than I did directions to the site."

"The text is carved into the benches and totally unreadable. You can't learn what you can't read. It's no surprise that no one can remember it. "

In spite of the fact that the sixteen-foot sculpture my students speak of sits adjacent to one of the busiest intersections in the city and at the entrance of a highly concentrated residential area, their comments represent how they perceived Wilmington's 1898 Memorial Park. Completed in 2008 and visible from the banks of the Cape Fear River, the installation is composed of six cast-bronze oars and several "reflection" benches. The students had visited the park to fulfill the "evaluating the historical landscape" assignment for my African American literature course that requires them to identify, research, and visit officially designated historic sites. The sites they selected had to connect to African American history and culture, in addition to the literary period we are studying. In this class, the historical spectrum covers writing from the 1600s to 1940.

It seems to me that the students encounter a historical landscape rooted in a kind of nostalgia that the fugitive slaves whose stories we read in class, and their descendants for that matter, would not be able to relate to. In the three years I've been assigning this project, a common sentiment often emerges in my students' writing. They begin to see more clearly Wilmington's various gestures to its Colonial and Confederate past. For example, downtown is littered with Civil War monuments, and people travel far and wide to witness the annual re-enactments of the fall of Fort Fisher. They also point out that, in their limited time in the city (usually around four years), the 1898 massacre gets no mention in the annual cultural festivals and ceremonies. In other words, the city does not claim that history in the same way it embraces its other uprisings and rebellions. This particular event seems to have little place in the story the city tells of itself to the rest of the nation. Sometimes in these discussions we explore possible alternative themes, such as what a re-enactment of emancipation might look like, or what an open-ended "Best of Wilmington" celebration would entail. Alas, we must deal with what is.

As I have said, students come to these conclusions on their own, after they have been informed by African American perspectives. Alongside the voices of famous freedom fighters like Frederick Douglass and Sojourner Truth, they read the work of North Carolina natives, such as Harriet Jacobs, David Walker, and Charles Chesnutt. Then, I send them out to study the region and city's historical landscape to interpret it for themselves. For the most part, they raise questions and approach these monuments and plaques with empathy for the lesser-known and lesser-celebrated people involved.

Still, my first reaction to the "I nearly missed it" responses from this year's crop of students was one of disappointment. I held high hopes for this insightful group of juniors and seniors because they always come to class — well, *most* of them do — with a delightful dose of inquiry and awareness mixed with conviction, an intellectual concoction that comes around (collectively) only every other year, it seems. Why didn't they bother to find out that the memorial is situated less than a block from the site where it is believed the first murder of the 1898 riot took place? Furthermore, why couldn't they see beyond the rundown houses that surround the memorial or draw the connection between the city's economic priorities and the state of the neighborhood?

Eventually, I have to recognize that I hadn't really equipped them to apply that level of intersectional analysis. And I have to admit that, although they said similar things about the seeming remoteness of certain cemeteries and highway markers, I am especially sensitive to their comments about the 1898 Memorial Park. It is in my neighborhood.

181

I chose to live in this particular part of downtown Wilmington because it is a predominately African American community. When I moved here, I was bone-deep tired of negotiating the white space that was the Florida college town where I attended graduate school. I wanted the comfort of being surrounded by black families, schoolchildren who reminded me of my nieces and nephews, and brown-faced merchants in my everyday life. I rented a townhouse and was happy to get it at a steal of a price. More importantly, this place would make me feel at home.

So, the 1898 Memorial Park is not the edge of town *for me*. But if you reside near the UNCW campus, as most students do, you drive to downtown through the city's center, not around the Martin Luther King Jr. highway connector that passes by the park.

Perception is reality. Driving into my part of the neighborhood means driving *away* from nearly everything else, including grocery stores, banks, and libraries. I also had to acknowledge that the students' reaction to the memorial was similar to something I'd experienced my first years here.

There is another memorial site in my community. I noticed it soon after I moved here, but its meaning and significance eluded me for some time. I first saw it during the summer of 2009. The neighborhood was still new to me and I would easily get disoriented driving along its one-way streets and winding roads that would suddenly change names after a bend or a stop sign. Although I relied heavily on the GPS attached to my windshield, I would feel a sense of relief when I got to the corner of Rankin and Eighth streets, because there it would be, another neighborhood monument signaling that I was close to my new home.

Initially, I thought it was an oddly placed leftover Christmas decoration: two small heart-shaped Mylar balloons—one red, the other purple—attached to a tiny brown teddy bear, with white artificial flowers surrounding it. All of this was anchored to a cement trashcan. Judging by its design and proximity to the children's playground, I guessed the can belonged to the city's parks and recreation department.

After a few months, the decorative display became as much a part of the landscape to me as the other everyday elements: When I pulled my car up alongside the wooden frame shotgun houses that line the street, or if I stopped at the corner store with the hand-painted sign, there it sat just beyond the circle of men who always stood together talking and laughing on the sidewalks in front of the houses. Or I would see the white polyester petals flapping in the wind, as if waving the children along when they crossed the street going to and from the park.

But one late summer day it was not there. Then it reappeared and I tried to pay better attention. The month was November. It disappeared again the next August. The same cycle happened for several years: The display was gone, then it was back with some different or newer-looking items. Finally, I gathered the nerve to ask Mr. Vincent about it. He was one of the older men who always waved back to me when I sat at the stoplight by the store.

"Oh that? Everybody knows Old Ms. Gladys puts it out every year for her great-grandparents, and other people come along and add stuff to it." A cigarette dangled dangerously from the tip of his lips as he spoke. His slight stutter made me miss my brother George. "Her father's people went m-m-missing in the 1898 killings. They hid her grandfather—he was a little boy then—at a white lady's house and never came back for him. Bodies never found either. Naw, that aint Christmas, darling. What you see there is the evidence of things unforgotten."

MARLON RACHQUEL MOORE fancies herself a poet and creative writer. In her day job, she does research in Southern culture and African American LGBTQ studies. Her work has appeared in academic journals and essay collections, including *Critical Insight* and *Sexuality, Religion and the Sacred*. Her book *In the Life and In the Spirit: Homoerotic Spirituality in African American Literature* was published in 2014.

Coup
(Wilmington, NC)

MICHAEL WHITE

Everyone goes for their evening walk
next to the Cape Fear's roiled and dented current
sidling past, as little rivulets

of melting praline ice cream drip down the sides
of the waffle cone I'm usually holding here.
Last Sunday, Sophia spotted a longnosed gar —

with delicate, attenuated bowsprit —
ghosting upstream just beside this wharf.
We followed it. How well the river fits

the city — white stone facing the tea-black tide —
the gutted ribs of hulls, sunk bones of piers
half risen once again on the other side.

Not much has changed, I think. Sometimes I imagine
10 November, 1898 —
the thud of a rifle butt at 8 a.m.

on the door of the *Daily Record.* Post election
Thursday morning. Colonel Waddell backed
by his white mob. You have to expect someone

would knock down lanterns, someone find a match.
The pop and whoosh of upper story windows —
flurries of sparks — then suddenly the crash . . .

You have to imagine cheers, their soaring hearts.
Therefore the march on Brooklyn — the colored section
whites called "darktown" — where, within an hour

a shout a shot a fusillade let fly
on a group of blacks on the porch of Walker's Store.
Some died where they fell, the others ran away,

but the infantry was called out anyway;
and Captain James, on the 4th Street Bridge to Brooklyn,
told his machine gun squad to "shoot to kill,"

and neighborhood churches, parks, and black-owned houses
everywhere were targets. Panic spread
from block to block like a sheet of wind-fanned flame.

Dan Wright was burned out, forced to run the gauntlet —
forty guns let loose at his back while his
wife, pleading, watched. Josh Halsey, trapped at last,

was forced to run the gauntlet — forty guns
"tore off the top of his head," as someone said,
while his young daughter watched. Imagine a woman

peering out through the drawn blinds of her living
room, as every prayer she had ever known
flits in and out of her mind . . . Her baby cries,

as just outside, the horse-drawn Gatling crew
takes aim: each burst of rounds like the Holy Ghost,
like the hieroglyphs of stars. So everyone who

could run, ran — four thousand women and children
exiled into swamps and graveyards. Dante
sang of "blackened waters" — city of "wretches

boiled in pitch" — and so Brooklyn became.
By 4 p.m., Waddell was declared mayor.
By 5 — gunmetal sundown — what it was

was ghost town: rubble of houses burning, crackle
of sniper fire, a pall of black smoke drifting
down the river. Some of the wounded crawled

beneath their own homes — and were found by the stench
days later. Twenty-five workers, picked off near
the railroad yard, were buried there in a ditch.

But most were left in plain sight: manifestos,
love notes to the future. Streetpole lynchings.
Rigored bodies lying in pools of blood.

"When we turned him over, Misto Niggah
had a look o' s'prise on his face!" one said.
And what it had been, now no longer was —

its bricklayers and drayers, its stevedores
and laundresses — no longer was. No one
came back. And yet it is so beautiful here:

the whole dusk taken in, the whole dusk given
back again, as livid strokes of cloud
and drawbridge laved across the bronze-green dark.

One of the last men killed, that night, was killed
right here, on Water Street. Two white men claimed
an unnamed black had "sassed" them. Therefore they shot him;

therefore they "tossed his body off the dock,"
where fathers and daughters ramble, and lovers talk,
and everyone goes for their evening walk.

MICHAEL WHITE has taught since 1994 at the University of North Carolina at Wilmington, where he currently chairs the creative writing department. His most recent books are the poetry collection *Vermeer in Hell* (winner of the Lexi Rudnitsky Editors Prize) and a memoir, *Travels in Vermeer*. He has published poetry and prose in *The Paris Review, The New Republic, The Missouri Review, The Kenyon Review,* and *The Best American Poetry.*

Views in Fiction

The Future Behind Me

An excerpt from a novel-in-progress

EMILY COLIN

[*Author's Note: Silas Paddington struggles with his conscience—and his sense of self—following a traumatic incident with his mentor, David, when the two were serving as army chaplains in Iraq. The reader doesn't know exactly what happened with—or to—David; this is a secret that Silas isn't ready to share. The encounter affected Silas profoundly, spurring him to leave the priesthood and retreat to his family's cottage in Wrightsville Beach.*]

I AM HAVING AN IDENTITY CRISIS.

This is nothing new, but my ongoing sense of ennui is augmented by the New Year's Eve gathering to which Kate has dragged me. I have nothing against the party, *per se*—the food is delicious, the people are decent conversationalists, and Abby and Birch have gone out of their way to make me feel welcome.

Still, I would've been perfectly happy—and certainly less stressed—at home, eating a frozen pizza and watching the ball drop. I told Kate this, but I don't think she believed me. In fact, I'm reasonably certain that she saw it as an act of charity to include me in her and Eduardo's plans for the evening. So, here I am, nibbling on stuffed mushrooms and trying to figure out how to behave now that I'm not Father Paddington anymore.

I was a priest for eight years and an army chaplain for two. That's how everyone knew me, whether I was wearing my collar or dressed in sweatpants, raking the yard. It's been a long time since I was just Silas, minus all the baggage that comes with priesthood. One on one, I don't tend to notice the difference so much. But here, in a room full of strangers, it's clear. No one is plying me with casseroles or getting me in a corner to confess their marital problems. No one's apologizing for swearing in front of me, like the guys in my unit always did, or asking my opinion about moral dilemmas—you know, what would Jesus do? And for sure, no one's confessing their desperate desire to escape their latest deployment or their inability to reconcile the act of gunning down an insurgent with their commitment to being a good Catholic.

It's not so much that I miss any of these things. In fact, I'd be happy if I never had to accept another chipped beef casserole or listen to Mrs. McConnell describe her inappropriate lust for the handyman ever again, much less all the rest of it. Still, in the absence of these types of interactions, and minus the camaraderie and adrenaline rush of combat—infused with a healthy dose of drudgery and more than my unit's fair share of tragedy—I have no idea how to conduct myself. So I hold my little plate, and I eat my stuffed mushrooms, and I try to act regular, like I used to.

The problem is, it's been too long. I have been in a religious brotherhood and I have been in a war and I am not Silas Paddington, eager Yale Divinity School graduate, anymore. I remember that guy's bright-eyed enthusiasm, his shiny-new-penny attitude toward saving the world, but it's through the proverbial glass darkly. Now, it's like all my feelings are wrapped in cotton batting. They're there, but muted, and if I really want to, I can pretend they don't exist.

As for my past, I left that behind in New Haven with my late-night library hours, in Virginia with my congregation and my brother, and in Iraq. The only piece I've hung onto is ten miles down the road in Wrightsville

Beach—my family's weather-beaten old cottage, dwarfed by the McMansions that flank it on either side. Every morning, I wake up and I watch the sun rise and I hope that things will be different. Once upon a time, I would have prayed. But that was then, this is now, and I don't pray anymore.

Now, of course, I am free. And I am terrified.

In the midst of this chaos, something about Rae gives me pause. I feel it from the first instant I see her, when we're standing in the doorway trading lines from Lewis Carroll. She isn't wearing makeup, or fancy clothes. She isn't dressed to impress, but she gets my attention and holds it anyhow. After my years in the ministry, I've become a decent judge of people. I have a feel for them, and Rae emanates a purity I haven't sensed in a long time. She seems *good,* and my entire being gravitates toward that like a light-starved plant toward the sun. It's not physical, at least not predominantly. Once upon a time I would have said it was spiritual. Now, who knows. All I can tell you is that for the few moments I talk with her, there in the doorway and again in the kitchen, I feel like things might be okay, and just maybe, I will be too.

All of which is to say that when Rae saves me from the talkative academic at her parents' New Year's Eve party, at first I'm relieved. The guy won't go away, so Rae takes me by the hand and pulls me out of the noisy living room. "Tea?" she says, towing me toward the kitchen like it's the most natural thing in the world.

Something shifts inside me then, wakes up and looks around. There are people everywhere, food and noise and music, but all I can think of is the feel of her warm fingers around mine. "Sure," I say, and let her lead the way.

Abby is in the kitchen, arranging sprigs of mint on a platter of chocolate-covered strawberries. "Want one?" she says when she sees us.

We shake our heads in unison. Rae says, "We're getting tea. Trying to escape from the madding crowd, and all that."

"*Uh-huh*. Well, don't be antisocial for *too* long." She smiles at us and heads back toward the living room, the strawberries balanced on one hand and a bottle of champagne in the other.

"That's directed at you, not me," Rae says. She opens a cabinet and stands on tiptoe, trying to reach something on one of the upper shelves.

I try not to stare at the way her breasts mold to the soft material of her sweater, how a pale stripe of stomach is revealed when she stretches her arms above her head. "What is?" I say, and pride myself on the fact that my voice comes out evenly.

"Abby's comment. She knows I hate parties. I'd much rather be in here drinking tea with you than dealing with all that." She waves her hand in the direction of the living room, from which the Violent Femmes, laughter, and raised voices are emanating at an impressive decibel level.

"Glad to oblige," I say, looking away as she manages to get hold of whatever she was looking for. It turns out to be a box of orange blossom tea.

"This okay?" she asks.

"Sure," I say again. I watch as she assembles the tea, pulling the mugs out of the cabinet, setting an honest-to-goodness kettle on to boil, heating milk in the microwave. "Abby seems nice," I venture, for want of something else to say.

"Oh, she is." Rae pulls a giant container of honey out of what must be the pantry.

"Have she and your dad been married long?"

"Since I was sixteen. So, twelve years. My mom died when I was four, so Abby's the closest thing I have to one."

"I didn't mean to pry," I say as she pours honey from the mammoth jar into a small pitcher and starts digging in the cabinet over the stove for something.

"You're not. I don't remember my mom. And Abby's great. We get along really well."

The microwave dings, and she extracts the milk, then goes back to rummaging in the cabinet again. Whatever it is, it must be buried. Either that, or she's just not tall enough to reach it. The sweater is lovely, but tight. And short. In desperation I say, "Can I help you find something?"

"There's a tray up here," she says. "It's white . . . I was going to put the tea stuff on it, but I don't see it anywhere."

"Let me look." I step closer. She smells like suntan lotion, even though it's the middle of winter. I find the tray in record time and hand it to her. "This one?" I say, stepping away as soon as is polite.

"Yep. Thanks." She arranges everything—mugs of tea, honey, milk, spoons—on the tray and leads the way to what turns out to be a sun porch, complete with wicker furniture and a daybed. It's cold out here, but Rae bustles around turning on a couple of space heaters. "Sit, sit," she says, gesturing at one of the couches.

I obey, cupping my hands around my mug of tea. She sits down next to me and doctors hers, adding milk and honey. *"Mmmm,"* she says after she takes a sip. "Perfection."

We sit for a moment, savoring the silence. Then she says, "Thanks for coming tonight."

"Thanks for having me. Really. I don't know a lot of people in Wilmington. Kate probably told you—I just moved here a little while ago."

I expect she'll ask about my tour in Iraq next—most people do—and brace myself for the awkwardness that's bound to ensue. I won't talk about what happened over there, not to fellow veterans and certainly not to a stranger. In fact I'd be thrilled if I could forget every second of it, above and beyond what I've already lost, but that isn't likely to happen. Not when I wake up seeing blood on my hands and devastation behind my eyes. Not when I look around every day and realize that the bedrock on which I built my life was quicksand, that my faith was a joke and God was nothing. In the middle of the night I can still hear David's voice, his lazy laughter curling into the air like smoke. *Are you going to stop me? Are you going to save her?* And then, when I couldn't, *Coward. . . .*

As if I need his accusations to remind me, I think, gulping the scalding tea. As if I'll ever forget what I am, who I turned out to be.

But Rae doesn't ask about the war. Instead she says, "I'm sorry Kate flashed you."

This is so unexpected that I choke on my tea and start coughing. When I can breathe again, I say, "It was dark, and she was running. I didn't see much. Plus Eduardo made her get dressed. I think he was embarrassed."

"I know he was," Rae says, and now she is laughing, a sweet childlike laugh that banishes David's voice to the furthest reaches of my mind, where it belongs. "Were you?"

"No," I admit. "I was . . . taken by surprise."

Rae laughs harder. "That's one way of putting it."

"Why did she do that?"

"Oh, Kate . . . I guess she thought you hadn't seen a naked woman in a long time, so she figured she'd be the first. What did she call it? An act of public service."

"Huh," I say, looking sideways at Rae, who has her legs curled up under her and is cradling her tea in one hand. She doesn't seem sexual anymore, or threatening. In fact she seems like a friend, and Lord knows I could use one of those right about now. "How thoughtful of her. Too bad the sun had gone down, and she was moving so quickly. Alas, my purity remains untarnished."

"I'll have to tell Kate," Rae says, smiling widely. "She'll be heartbroken."

"No, please don't. Then she'll be tempted to do it again, or worse." I like Kate, but honestly I find her a bit overwhelming. Eduardo is more my speed—and Rae, who is adding even more honey to her tea, stirring with as much concentration as if she's preparing a potion for Professor Snape. Rae, who wants to do some good in the world and hasn't asked me anything about Iraq.

"So," she says. "Kate says you grew up coming to Wilmington?"

"My family has a house at Wrightsville Beach. It's just a cottage, nothing like these giant pastel monstrosities they're building now. My brother Martin and I used to spend every day on the beach. It wasn't nearly so commercial then," I say, thinking about how we used to run wild up and down the strand. We'd come home at night coated in sand like a couple of cutlets. My mom would make us use the outdoor shower before we were allowed to set foot inside, but we always wound up with sand in our beds anyhow. It drove her crazy.

The road from there to here has been long and twisted. My mom is long since dead, Martin is married with three kids, and I am best defined by what I am not: a soldier, a minister to the sick and lost, a believer in something bigger than myself, something good. "I guess Thomas Wolfe is right. You really can't go home again," I say, chugging the tea like it's whiskey and wishing for the first time that I was drinking tonight.

Rae leans toward me, her eyes on my face. "Is that why you came back? To find your way home?"

It's an intimate question, and I'm not prepared to answer it. So I don't, and in the silence that falls between us I hear the people in the living room start yelling and cheering. There's the pop of a champagne cork, and shouts of "Happy New Year!"

"Happy New Year," Rae says with less exuberance but equal sincerity, clinking her mug against mine.

Before I can overthink it, I lean forward and kiss her. It's quite possible that I'll regret this later, but just at the moment, I don't care. There have got to be some fringe benefits to walking away from your life, and kissing Rae may well be one of them. She tastes like honey. Her lips are warm under mine, from her body heat and the tea.

I'm long out of practice, but I can't imagine kissing's something you forget how to do. However, I don't think this is a fair trial run, given Rae's response. She doesn't push me away, but she doesn't kiss me back, either. In fact, she just sits there, clutching her tea. I think she would have been less surprised if I'd smacked her.

"Why did you do that?" she says when I draw back, blinking like an owl that's been deposited in bright sunlight. I realize it's the question I asked her earlier, about Kate.

"Because I wanted to," I say. For once, this is the simple, uncomplicated truth. "Happy New Year to you too, by the way," I tell her, and then Birch is calling both of us, and the moment is gone.

EMILY COLIN is the author of *The Memory Thief* and a forthcoming novel (title to be announced). She is the associate director of DREAMS of Wilmington, a nonprofit dedicated to providing youth in need with high-quality arts programming. Previously, she served as the editor-in-chief of Coastal Carolina Press, the organizer of a Coney Island tattoo and piercing show, and an itinerant violinist.

Ouroboros

Adapted from the forthcoming novel,
The Sheltering Abyss: Beyond Cape Fear

DANIEL NORRIS

"BY THE POWER VESTED IN ME by the great state of North Carolina, I now pronounce you husband and wife."

Amy and Cameron faced each other and held hands as the white-haired female magistrate read vows from an index card. They had decided to marry just the day before. And now, two days since Amy had shown up at Cameron's parents' house, they were married.

The magistrate stood awkwardly until she remembered to add, "You may kiss the bride."

Cameron and Amy kissed and then stood apart to look at each other.

Amy wore a simple cream-colored, baby-doll dress made of sheer lace and tulle. Her shoulders were covered by a matching gossamer-thin, short-waisted cashmere sweater.

Cameron couldn't take his eyes off her for the hour-long trip from White Lake to Wilmington. He had never seen her look so beautiful. He thought it was a combination of the outfit and the way she seemed to glow with the light of being pregnant. It overwhelmed his senses. He was surprised he wasn't even at least a little bit nervous about their impending marriage. They decided to do it in Wilmington. No reason other than today they would be there looking for rings.

At his grandma's insistence, Cameron wore one of his daddy's ties, a white dress shirt, black belt, and dark gray pants. He donned a pair of oxford shoes. Also borrowed from his daddy. They were slightly too large.

Earlier that morning, he and Amy picked out their rings. Amy suggested an unpretentious little jewelry shop that she had been to before at the Cotton Exchange on Front Street. The jeweler and an assistant pulled out at least three hundred different rings before Amy eventually said, "That one. That's the one." Cameron politely agreed. "Perfect."

The two rings were matching platinum bands. The groom's ring slightly wider than the bride's. A single faceted ruby marked the eye of a snake carved into the band. The design ran the circumference of the ring. The snake's mouth was open and it appeared to be eating its own tail. Amy told the jeweler she was familiar with the symbol.

"It is the ouroboros," Amy explained to Cameron.

"And?" Cameron said.

"Oh. Well. It symbolizes birth, rebirth. The cycle of life and death. And, *uh,* primordial unity. Something that has always existed and is so basic and pervasive, it cannot be destroyed."

"*Whoa.* That is deep."

"I like the symbolism," she said. "Many cultures have adopted it. I think the first were the Egyptians."

Cameron said, "Well you've done your homework. But I do like the ring." Cameron rolled it around on the ring finger of his left hand. "It feels comfortable on my finger. I'll wear it all the time."

Amy giggled like a teenager as she looked down at her hand. "It feels just right. No need to cut it down. It's perfect."

The jeweler said, "Very good. It matches your caduceus pendant nicely."

Amy looked down at her pendant and instinctively grabbed it. Hiding it from view. "It's not a caduceus," she said. "It is the Rod of Asclepius. A symbol . . . of . . ." Her voice monotone. The pendant had been a constant reminder to her during her darkest moments that healing was possible, that she once again would be able to trust and love.

Cameron noticed that Amy had blushed dramatically, her face and neck now completely red.

The jeweler noticed her discomfort at the mention as well and quickly added, "Oh. I'm sorry."

Amy shook her head and grabbed the edge of the glass counter to steady her self. "Oh. No need to apologize. It's a family heirloom. A bit of a good-luck talisman. It is my . . ." Her voice faded out again as her words trailed off into an indecipherable gurgle. She released the pendant and then seemed to quickly resurface.

"Where were we?" she asked.

The jeweler continued, "Er. Ah. The pendant, I mean the rings. These rings are not adjustable. The design would not allow them to be cut down. You two are very lucky."

"Why's that?" Cameron said. He wanted to give Amy a breather from the task at hand.

The jeweler added politely, "Those two rings have been here for as long as we've been in business. I believe they came from an estate sale. Obviously they were once a cherished heirloom."

Cameron said, "Not so cherished they didn't mind selling them off in an estate sale." But no sooner had he said it than he realized it was a bit brusque. He thought to himself, *But what people hold dear changes over time.*

Cameron paid the jeweler for the rings and he and Amy left the shop hand in hand. It was eleven o'clock. They considered walking the few blocks to the courthouse but thought better of it. Choosing rings had been more exhausting than Amy realized. She wanted to conserve enough energy to last the rest of the day.

"Your carriage awaits, Madame," Cameron said as he opened the passenger door of the car. They drove three blocks to the courthouse for their civil ceremony.

In the offices of the New Hanover County magistrate's office, the ceremony was over. Two willing office workers had served as witnesses. Even though the register of deeds was only a block down Third Street, they hopped into the car again. Cameron insisted that Amy not overexert herself. At almost eight and a half months, she was glad to be chauffeured. She was already exhausted and it was not even noon.

After their wedding license was recorded, and a quick lunch at the little German restaurant behind the Cotton Exchange, he and Amy decided to make their way back to White Lake. It would be after three when they got back to the cottage. And Amy wanted to take a little nap and then get ready before they went over to Cameron's parents' house for a celebratory supper.

She hoped the long talk they had the other night helped Cameron understand what she'd been through. He seemed to understand that she was a different person. The same but different. She couldn't stop thinking about the look of surprise on his face when she turned around. She hated dropping that bombshell on him right then. She wanted this more than anything she had ever wanted. He made her happy. She felt like she made him happy too.

DANIEL NORRIS designs and writes books about local history. He is an avid photographer, graphic designer, biology teacher, and videographer. Born and raised in the Wilmington area, he can trace his ancestry back to the pirate, Blackbeard. He struggles daily not to wreak havoc among the southward sailing vessels that ply the Intracoastal Waterway behind his house.

About the Cover

The cover illustration for *27 Views of Wilmington* is the work of Chapel Hill writer and artist Daniel Wallace. He has illustrated the book covers for Eno Publishers's entire "27 Views" series, including local anthologies for Hillsborough, Chapel Hill, Raleigh, Asheville, Durham, Charlotte, and Greensboro. He is also the author of *Big Fish, Ray in Reverse, The Watermelon King,* and many other novels and short stories. He is the author and illustrator of *The Cat's Pajamas,* a children's book published by Inkshares.

Award-winning Books from Eno Publishers

27 Views of Greensboro
The Gate City in Prose & Poetry
INTRODUCTION BY MARIANNE GINGHER
$15.95/200 pages

27 Views of Charlotte
The Queen City in Prose & Poetry
INTRODUCTION BY JACK CLAIBORNE
$14.95/226 pages

27 Views of Raleigh
The City of Oaks in Prose & Poetry
INTRODUCTION BY WILTON BARNHARDT
$15.95/224 pages

27 Views of Durham
The Bull City in Prose & Poetry
INTRODUCTION BY STEVE SCHEWEL
$15.95/216 pages

27 Views of Asheville
A Southern Mountain Town in Prose & Poetry
INTRODUCTION BY ROB NEUFELD
$15.95/216 pages

27 Views of Chapel Hill
A Southern University Town in Prose & Poetry
INTRODUCTION BY DANIEL WALLACE
$16.50/240 pages

27 Views of Hillsborough
A Southern Town in Prose & Poetry
INTRODUCTION BY MICHAEL MALONE
$15.95/216 pages
Gold IPPY Book Award, Best Anthology
Gold Eric Hoffer Book Award, Culture

Chapel Hill in Plain Sight
Notes from the Other Side of the Tracks
DAPHNE ATHAS
$16.95/246 pages

Undaunted Heart
The True Story of a Southern Belle & a Yankee General
SUZY BARILE
$16.95/238 pages
Silver IPPY Book Award, Best Regional Nonfiction

Brook Trout & the Writing Life
The Intermingling of Fishing & Writing in a Novelist's Life
CRAIG NOVA
$15.95/152 pages

Rain Gardening in the South
Ecologically Designed Gardens for Drought,
Deluge & Everything in Between
HELEN KRAUS & ANNE SPAFFORD
$19.95/144 pages
Gold Book Award, Garden Writers Association
Silver Book Award, Garden Writers Association
Silver Benjamin Franklin Book Award
Honorable Mention, Eric Hoffer Book Award

Eno's books are available at your local bookshop and from
www.enopublishers.org